PRAISES FOR UP FROM THE BOTTOM

Up From the Bottom is a timeless account of enduring struggles, disappointments, and setbacks balanced by perseverance, sacrifice, and hope. It is an exceedingly honest and captivating memoir which unabashedly points to the power of loving-kindness and redemption—a testament to the unconquerable soul.

Colonel David Rabb , LCSW

Enlightened reading not only for people of color, who are quite familiar with pain and oppression, but people who have struggled and at times allowed self-doubt to seep within. *Up From the Bottom* truly illustrates that light will prevail.

Terence Fitzgerald, Ph.D., M.Ed., MSW

Truly grateful for the gift of this compelling story. It is a testament to the power of turning tragedy into triumph, resilience, and most important, forgiveness! This is a powerful story of one man's journey of overcoming adversity against all odds.

Donna L. Cook, Ph.D., MSN, BSN
Psychiatric Clinical Nurse Specialist

A pathfinder of courage and resilience. In this compelling memoir, the reader will travel with the narrator exploring how community, love, and courage molds one's worldview, and how faith can pull you from the deepest abyss. "Ask, and it shall be given you; seek, and ye shall find; knock, and it shall be opened unto you ..." (Matthew 7:7)

Jose E. Coll, Ph.D.

Isaac Ford's story of his life is a riveting account of the limitless possibilities of the human spirit and its ability to triumph over trauma, adversity, and discrimination. Despite a turbulent childhood and mistreatment from multiple systems—family, employment, military, and law enforcement—Isaac Ford did not let feeling "less than," for most of his life derail him from achieving his dreams. Instead, he used "his village" of extended family, friends, and colleagues to propel him forward. Through sheer will, unimaginable tenacity, and God's grace, he overcame adversity to become the man he is today: self-assured, self-less, and driven to be a guiding light for others by sharing his story. For those who are broken or feel worn down by the weight of the world, their counselors, teachers, and mentors, this book is a must-read.

Jennifer Simpson, Ed.D.

A compelling and inspirational recount of triumph over the adverse circumstances that plagues many of our communities. Replete with examples of a man's indomitable spirit to live a life of integrity and overcome unspeakable life events. An absolute must-read to equip all committed to mentoring youths to live a life with integrity and overcome personal tragedy.

Colonel William Gillespie, U.S. Marine Corps, Retired
Alpha Phi Alpha Fraternity Inc. President, San Diego Chapter

Isaac left no stone unmourned and with each heartfelt discovery, there is a sincere and open healing path to recovery. This is a book that should be read by anyone who landed in the potholes of life, stuck in childhood chaos, or has experienced unmentionable disappointments by the people who are supposed to love you; and you are still standing, growing and positively impacting the lives of others.

Dr. Kimberly Finney, Psy. D., ABPP, ABMP

The reading of Isaac Ford Jr.'s story is captivating. He suffered trauma and challenges that had the potential to destroy his life. This story can teach others in the same type of situations how to make it despite their past. Although we think we go through life unscathed, the "chance encounter" made it clear that all was not well. The cathartic nature of writing and talking about the stories of our lives can help us to soar even higher.

Yvonette Powell, Ed. D, LCSW

UP FROM THE BOTTOM

A Memoir

Isaac Ford Jr., MSW

UP FROM THE BOTTOM
A Memoir

for Azalia Ford

CONTENTS

INTRODUCTION

In April 2018, while attending the 50ᵗʰ Anniversary of the National Association of Black Social Workers (NABSW) Conference in San Diego, California, I had a remarkable encounter with a woman from my distant past, a lifetime away during my childhood in Augusta, Georgia. This extraordinary meeting and the powerful reaction it evoked, moved me to finally put into words something that I have struggled with for more than four decades. My improbable story began in Washington, D.C., but the people and experiences that had the most impact on my life were from Augusta in a segregated section of the city affectionately called "The Bottom." It was here that I learned the value of the extended family: values, work ethic, character, respect, the power of faith, and resilience. This village, which included my maternal grandparents, aunts, uncles, cousins, and the black church, helped me survive tragedy in my childhood and prepared me for the daunting challenges that awaited me outside of the Bottom. It is my hope that my story will inspire others to believe that anything is possible with hard work, determination, and faith, regardless of where you start in life.

AUTHOR'S NOTE

In the interest of protecting individuals' privacy, the author has changed the names of some characters.

The more you praise and celebrate your life,
the more there is in life to celebrate.
—Oprah Winfrey

CHANCE ENCOUNTER

T HE NABSW CONFERENCE attracts the best and brightest from around the world and focuses on every aspect of social work and advocacy but through an unapologetically Afrocentric lens.

It was the third day of the conference, and I was looking forward to attending two seminars scheduled in the Bay Tower. The first was scheduled at 10:30 a.m., the second at 1:00 p.m. that afternoon. As I entered the elevator of the Sheraton San Diego Hotel and Marina, I was greeted by two beautiful African American women eloquently dressed in brightly colored African attire, looking like African royalty. Throughout the week-long conference, attendees wear elaborate traditional African clothing and greet each other with warm traditional African greetings.

"Are you ladies enjoying the conference and San Diego?" I asked as the elevator door closed.

"Yes, we are, thank you," they said on one accord. "How about you?"

"I always enjoy attending NABSW conferences."

The conversation continued as the elevator reached the first floor. We exited as the doors opened, stopping in the center of the hotel's lobby to await the start of the next seminars. The beautiful San Diego Bay was in full view directly behind us through the lobby's front entrance. Dozens of sailboats adorned with brightly colored sails could be seen traversing the picturesque San Diego Bay as well as tourist boats filled with tourists. We continued our small talk. I found out that they were from Atlanta, Georgia (where I had family living), and that one of them worked in Augusta early in her career as a Child Protective Services (CPS) caseworker.

"Really?" I said surprised at how we were connecting.

"What is your family's name?" she asked.

"It's a unique name. Boler."

"I'm certain I worked with someone in your family."

By now, I was very curious as to who she might have worked with, especially as a CPS social worker. My wheels were really turning at this point, and I dug deeper.

"The person you worked with, do you remember whether it were a male or female?"

She took a moment to think about it. "I'm sure it was a female."

I think we both knew at this point that there was going to be a big reveal.

"Was her name Mildred? Was it Myrtis?" I asked.

"No, I don't think so."

My maternal grandparents had five boys and five girls, and I had already narrowed the woman down to one of two sisters, my youngest aunt, or my mother.

Reluctantly, after a short pause, I summoned the courage and asked, "Was her name Lillie?"

"Yes, it was!" I took a moment to compose myself. "She was my mother," I said in a muffled, barely-audible voice. What was the likelihood of me meeting a woman from Atlanta in a San Diego hotel elevator, 2,000 miles away, who knew my mother four decades ago? It was surreal. I could see the shock on her face and her colleague's face having witnessed this incredible exchange. They both read my body language and noticed that I no longer had a poker face. The confident persona I usually project disappeared within seconds. Suddenly, I felt incredibly vulnerable, like I was naked standing in the middle of the hotel's lobby. An avalanche of raw, dormant emotions overcame me, as we stood there fixated on each other. I struggled to form the words but broke the awkward silence when I looked at her and said, "I'm him."

"Oh, my God!"

This lovely woman I met in the elevator less than ten minutes earlier turned out to be my CPS caseworker from four decades earlier. She was assigned to my family after I was stabbed at thirteen years old in the Delta Manor Housing Projects. She hugged me as tears streamed down my face. I didn't fully understand what had just happened. This incredible meeting triggered emotions that I struggled to comprehend. Curious conference attendees passed us, wondering what was going on. *Why here? Why now?* I wondered.

"How have you been, are you okay?" she asked.

It took a minute for me to compose myself. "I have done well by the grace of God."

Despite all I had seen, survived, and accomplished over the years, this ghost, this childhood trauma was still difficult for me to talk about. It was still my kryptonite. What were the odds that she and I would encounter each other forty years later at a conference for social workers of all places? Meeting each other had to be on par with the chances of getting struck by lightning or selecting six winning numbers in the lottery. As quickly as she appeared, she disappeared back into the throngs of conference attendees. I searched for her during the week and even contacted her chapter, hoping to reconnect and ask her about things I was never privy to, but we wouldn't meet again for the rest of the week. I knew this remarkable encounter was no coincidence. I believe this was God's way of telling me that He wanted me to share my improbable story, and by doing so, complete my own healing, something that was still very much a work-in-progress. At the same time, my painful childhood experience and my path since that time could be instructive, and help others who have experienced trauma and adversity to believe that they didn't have to be defined by what happened to them, instead they can draw strength and grow from those painful experiences.

The capacity for hope is the most significant fact of life. It provides human beings with a sense of destination and energy to get started.
—Norman Cousins

THE BEGINNING

MY MOTHER WAS beautiful, intelligent, strong-willed, fearless, and she danced to her own music. She was the sixth of ten children born in 1944 and raised in Augusta during The Great Depression. She was a war baby. My father was a brilliant man born and raised on a small farm in rural Birmingham, Alabama in 1937. He was the seventh of ten children. They were both from large families in the deep south, led by strong, hard-working fathers and very resourceful, loving mothers. My maternal grandfather retired from Augusta Iron and Steel Company as a truck driver. He supplemented the family's income with a firewood, ice delivery, and ice cream truck business. My paternal grandfather worked in the steel mills in Birmingham and supplemented the family's income by raising hogs, cattle, chickens, and growing cotton.

Hard work and Christian values were instilled by both families to each of their children and grandchildren. The world they grew up in was fraught with hardship, racism, and intolerance, so they had no choice but to be resilient and resourceful. My father was drafted into the army during the height of the Vietnam War, but due to his high scores, he served his entire enlistment stateside. My parents met while my father was stationed at Fort Gordon Army installation just outside of Augusta. He served as an army medic and rose to the rank of Specialist E-4 where he was assigned ambulance duty. Before my father met my mother, he was already engaged to his college sweetheart from Miles College in Alabama, but he fell in love with my mother while he was stationed at Fort Gordon. My father returned to Washington, D.C., following his enlistment and married his fiancé, but the marriage dissolved in less than a year. My mother was only seventeen when she had my older brother and my grandparents forbade her from taking him out of the state, so he was raised from a baby by my grandparents in Augusta. My father sent for my mother shortly after his short-lived marriage ended, and she moved to D.C. where she worked and sent my grandparents money to support my brother.

My sister was born soon after my mother arrived in D.C., and I was born a year and a half later. My parents had a very complex and volatile relationship. My father was madly in love with my mother, but he made the mistake of trying to control her. They fought often, largely because of his jealousy and insecurities. Perhaps it was because of their age difference—he was seven years older than her. At one point, he went as far as lightly sprinkling baby powder on the floor near the front and back door entrances of our apartment before going to work. This was his futile attempt to prevent my mother from leaving the house while he was away at work or on business. Of course, she was having none of it. She wanted to go and hang out with her friends, and so she did. During the summers, my mother flew my sister and me to Augusta to spend time with my grandparents, brother, and cousins. When her work schedule permitted, she accompanied us on trips to Augusta by passenger train. My father's family was also in D.C. He and his siblings followed his oldest sister, my aunt Onita there beginning in the mid 1950s during The Great Northward Migration. Still, my mother wanted us to know and engage with our Georgia family and to have that southern influence she grew up with.

While we lived in D.C., my father spent time with my sister and me, but our aunts filled in whenever possible, taking us on day trips to the monuments and other D.C. highlights. This would be the last time my father participated in our lives in any significant way. My parents eventually grew apart and separated for good in 1973. In the summer of 1973, we left D.C. and moved to Augusta. My sister was nine, and I was seven years old. My mother realized that she needed help raising us, and she had a large supportive family in Augusta that would help her. Augusta is Georgia's second largest city after it's capital, Atlanta. It lies across the Savannah River from North Augusta, South Carolina, and it's the home of the world famous Augusta National Golf Course, which hosts the Masters Golf Tournament—the Super Bowl of golf. The Augusta National has some of the most majestic fairways in the country and attracts some of the best golfers in the world.

James Brown, the Godfather of Soul, was born in South Carolina, but famously claimed the Garden City, Augusta, as his hometown. We moved to east Augusta, a segregated section of the city affectionately known as "The Bottom." The Bottom was the area east of East Boundary Street and was bordered by the Savannah River to the north and east, and by the CSX railroad yard to the south. Those living in the Bottom learned to live with mile-long train processions that were known to block all traffic traveling east and west, often stopping for up to an hour. Tragically, this included ambulances, fire trucks, and police cars. Countless lives were lost over the years because emergency vehicles were unable to reach the residents living east of the train tracks during emergencies. Our maternal grandparents lived a short one hundred yards away from us in a modest, three-bedroom brick home on Laney Circle. They owned their home as did many others in the Bottom, which included middle class, working class, and poor families often living across the street from each other.

Our apartment was on the 200 block of East Hale Street in the Delta Manor Housing Projects, a street that was always teeming with children playing from the end of school until dinnertime. Dun's Barbershop was four blocks away. It was the place where black men of every stature gathered to get a fresh haircut for church and pontificate about everything from politics to sports. I called it "The University" and looked forward to listening to the insightful discussions between men of all ages. The neighborhood beauty salon was next door, and it offered young girls and women an equally rich environment for enlightenment. The black-owned community grocery store, Quick Check, was on the other side of the barbershop and the only grocery store in the Bottom. If ever in a pinch, the owners would allow families to purchase items on credit until payday. By far, one of the busiest establishments in the Bottom was the Cool Spot Liquor Store. It was two hundred yards away from our apartment, just across Gwinnett Street. Too many residents from the Bottom frequented this establishment and business was always brisk.

The only thing good that ever came from this place was Shapiro beef sausage dogs from the snack truck that parked in the parking lot of the establishment. Hands down these were the best all-beef sausage dogs in the city. My mother would occasionally bring them home for my sister and me. They were loaded with diced onions, relish, and topped off with ketchup and mustard. Coney Island hot dogs had nothing on them. Mr. McDonald was a retired army veteran from the neighborhood who walked past our apartment daily on his way to Cool Spot. Sadly, his wife and teenage daughter would have to come looking for him each evening just before dark. They would often find him passed out in a ditch or in the grass next to Gwinnett Street. Neighborhood kids would sometimes tease him and poke him with sticks when they found him unconscious in the grass. Years later, I wondered what Mr. McDonald had seen and experienced, both growing up in the south and while fighting in South Vietnam. What dark secrets haunted him and how did his treatment as a scorned Vietnam veteran contribute to his alcoholism. Vietnam veterans didn't have the vast array of resources available to them as returning Desert Shield/Storm and Iraq and Afghanistan veterans have today. The country made a tragic mistake by not embracing them when they returned home from war.

There were no McDonald's, Burger King, Krystal's or Wendy's restaurants located in the Bottom. There were no major grocery store chains, banks, bakeries, ice cream parlors, nor were there clothing stores. This was in stark contrast to businesses located just two miles west of East Boundary, which was the dividing line for residents living in the Bottom. The Columbia Nitrogen Chemical Plant was a mile east of where we lived, much too close to Hornsby Elementary School and Sand Bar Ferry Junior High School to be healthy. Similar chemical plants are situated in black communities throughout the southeast, saturating the surrounding air and water with carcinogens. During peak production cycles, the toxic smell of chemical emissions could become so strong you could almost taste it in the air. James Brown had a popular nightclub called The Third World a half mile away on Gwinnett Street. He also owned Augusta's most popular black radio station, WRDW radio. I walked to school with my sister and other kids from Delta Manor each day, sometimes at my own peril. On more than one occasion, I would have to run home, trying to avoid the neighborhood twins who were waiting for me. They would take turns trying out the latest wrestling moves on me, including flying drop kicks. Bullying was a fact of life while growing up in Delta Manor, and I learned valuable life lessons from dealing with them that would prepare me for life outside of the Bottom.

In the beginning of my fourth grade year at W.S. Hornsby Elementary School, I was assigned to flag duty with several other classmates. We took pride in raising and folding the flag each morning and afternoon. On one fateful morning, while attempting to raise the flag, the chain on the flagpole got stuck, and after a slight tug, the 1,000-pound flag pole broke off at its rusted base and toppled over, landing on top of me. It felt like a car had rolled over me. My classmate barely escaped injury and ran to get help from teachers and office staff. It was a miracle that we weren't both killed. I sustained a bruised pelvis and a slight concussion and was hospitalized for observation, then released after two days. It seemed that I was a magnet for mishaps, dog bites, and stitches over a three-year period. We played hard in the Bottom. Wars with discarded roof shingles earned me a permanent forehead scar, and I lost my share of races against pissed off neighborhood dogs.

Everyone knew each other in the neighborhood, and if you screwed up, you could be sure your family would find out in record time. We were taught to respond to any adult with either *Yes, sir,* or *Yes, ma'am.* Ms. Millie, our next door neighbor, sold frozen red and grape Kool-Aid ice cups for ten cents, and the best bright red candy apples in the projects for twenty-five cents each from her back-porch store. She was an accomplished entrepreneur, selling kids snacks during the week and liquor to adults on Sundays. She was very nice to everyone. Ms. Pollard and her family lived on the other side of us. She was a beautiful spirit, always encouraging us and occasionally scolding my mother when she felt it was warranted, undaunted by the price she would have to pay for getting involved.

During the summers, we enjoyed free lunches from the Feed-A-Kid program at the Delta Manor Community Center. Those cold box lunches were a hit in the Bottom. We lined up to receive lunches packed in dry ice that included a sandwich, a piece of fruit, a juice cup, and milk. Government cheese made for great grilled cheese sandwiches, and in a pinch, my fallback snack was toast with butter and sugar sprinkled on top. My mother was a great cook, and I enjoyed her homemade spaghetti, fried chicken, hog maws, banana pudding, and sweet potato pies. Her sweet potato pies were so good that my brother and I would cut them in half and eat them in one sitting. When she didn't feel like cooking, my grandmother always had a place at her table for us. It was simple. If you worked, you were golden. So, working in the yard, cleaning up the car on Saturday, and doing odd jobs for neighbors brought you capitol. My grandparents instilled work ethic and character in all of us. Everyone in my family worked, and the men in my family provided for their families and stayed with them.

I can still smell my grandmother's delicious fried chicken, macaroni with extra sharp cheese, lima beans, collard greens, and flour bread made on top of the stove in a fifty-year-old cast iron skillet. For dessert, she made pound cake with the hard crust top, peach cobbler sweet enough to cause instant diabetes, Granny Smith apple pies, bread pudding, and my favorite, homemade fig preserves. To this day, I would pay fifty dollars a jar to anyone that can duplicate my grandmother's delicious fig preserves recipe. My grandparents' backyard was the Garden of Eden. The sweet smell of honeysuckles and magnolias, and the summer songs of cicadas waking from their long sleep permeated the summer afternoons. There was a Granny Smith apple tree, a peach tree, a pear tree, a fig tree, a grapevine fashioned under an old box-spring hoisted on five-foot poles, collard greens, cucumbers, fresh ripe tomatoes, and watermelons. It was here in this segregated community that I learned the value of extended family, "my village," which included my grandparents, a host of aunts, uncles, cousins, and, of course, my church family.

My mother's youngest brother, Sylvester, was a hometown football legend, receiving over fifty scholarship offers before graduating from Lucy Laney High School. He played at the University of Georgia, earning the Most Valuable Player trophy in the Peach Bowl. My uncle Mason owned a successful restaurant on the Hill. Richard owned a liquor store and night club on East Boundary Street, and Harold managed top restaurants on the west coast. Three of my aunts: Mildred, Evelyn, and Myrtis were career civil service workers at Gracewood State School and Hospital, and the youngest, Olivia, worked at University Hospital. "Daddy," as we called my grandfather, was a man of few words, but taught me discipline, work ethic, and respect. He was a very resourceful man, always building something in the backyard, and I enjoyed watching and helping him with his projects. He even built a swimming pool under the large weeping willow tree and a basketball court for the grandchildren. He also designed and built barbecue grills and beautiful flower pots, which to this day still adorn many yards throughout the Bottom. His entrepreneurial example inspired his children and grandchildren to start businesses that ranged from beauty salons, truck washing companies, barbecue businesses, advertising companies, and even a trucking company.

My grandfather, like all the men on my mother's side of the family, was an excellent cook too. He made homemade hash from stewed chicken necks, the best barbecue ribs and chicken, and homemade ice cream from ice, Carnation milk, rock salt, and hand-picked peaches from the backyard. He introduced me to delicacies like rabbit, racoon, venison, and squirrel. The fishing lunches were just as memorable as the actual fishing outings. Life was good, especially when we returned home with enough bream, bass, and crappie for a small fish fry. He made salmon croquettes and grits, and my favorite was grits and ham with red-eye gravy. If he and my grandmother were alive today, they could certainly have their own show on the cooking channel.

I have told you these things so that in me you may have peace. In this world you will have trouble. But take heart. I have overcome the world.
—John 16:33

TROUBLE ON EAST HALE STREET

O UR APARTMENT WAS burglarized twice within a two-year period. Nothing went unnoticed in Delta Manor Housing Projects, but I guess someone thought we had something in our modest apartment that they didn't have. Perhaps this was because when we moved in, my mother owned a beautiful gold 1973 Ford Elite with white interior. I will never forget how humiliated my mother was when it was repossessed in the middle of the day while everyone was sitting on their porch and the street was full of kids playing. The first break-in occurred while we were away. This intrusion was more about vandalism than anything else. Burglars ransacked our apartment and poured food into the goldfish bowl just for good measure. I was young, but I can remember feeling incredibly violated after finding all of my meager possessions strewn throughout my room and the hallway.

The second burglary took on a more ominous tone, because an intruder broke into our apartment while my sister and I were at home alone. My mother went out with friends that night, and whoever came to pick her up stood outside of our apartment blowing the horn and yelling at the top of his voice, "Hurry up, we are going to be late." That's not exactly the thing you want to do if you're trying to leave home and not broadcast your departure, especially in the projects. I guess someone was paying attention, and they assumed that when my mother left the apartment, it was empty. They were wrong. Within an hour of my mother leaving, I was awakened by a commotion in our kitchen, and I went to investigate because I was the man of the house. As I entered the kitchen, I was startled by a young black man about nineteen years old. After staring at each other for a second, he bolted past me nearly knocking me down. Instinctively, I called out to my sister as he ran past me. "Sis, lock your door! Somebody is in the house!"

I was probably eleven years old at the time and helpless to protect us, but I was going to try. Fortunately for us, a guardian angel was looking out for us that night (and many more nights to come) and the burglar ran out our front door. Out of concern for our safety, my grandfather installed makeshift safety devices for the apartment windows. Nailing the windows shut stopped the burglaries, but it also prevented the apartment from getting fresh air. Mom was a chain smoker, smoking a minimum of a pack a day back then. Our clothes were saturated with the smell of stale cigarette smoke. You could smell us before we walked into a room. As a result, I promised myself that when I grew up, no one would ever smoke in my home or cars. True to my word, no one has to this day.

In the early days, my mother paid for us to take piano lessons with Mrs. Rush, a music teacher that lived directly across the street from us. She wanted to expose us to things that could expand our horizons. She was fiercely protective of her children and did her best to support us on her own. I give her great credit for this, and I empathize with her and all single mothers who courageously take on the daunting task of being both mother and father. Mom would save money to take us horseback riding in Graniteville, S.C., and she bought us a brand new volume of World Book Encyclopedias, which I read every chance I had. The encyclopedias offered us an escape and helped foster dreams of a life outside of the projects, a life without limits. On Sundays, Mom would drive us to the Hill section of Augusta, because she wanted us to see how the "other half" lived. She always encouraged us to dream of a life outside of Delta Manor and the Bottom.

Poor blacks lived in certain sections of the Hill as well because they once worked as nannies, domestic workers, and gardeners for affluent whites living in the stately homes that dotted the Hill. Mom hated living in poverty, and she was frustrated that she was still struggling after having left Augusta. She realized that there was a caste system in the Bottom, and in life in general, and she didn't want us to be limited by it as she had been. She even took us on road trips to Atlanta, and she once drove us to Saint Augustine, Florida. I don't think I realized we were poor until I attended high school years later. She did the best she could with what she had, and our grandparents did their best to back her up. I cut neighbors' grass and raked leaves for extra money. Ms. Wallace, an old lady living in Laney Circle, would work me for hours in exchange for a crisp five dollar bill. My older brother worked for her until he was old enough to get other jobs. She called me my brother's name so often, I stopped correcting her and started answering to his name.

The housing project we lived in was built on the grounds of an expansive pecan orchard and the decades-old trees remained. Neighborhood boys threw large sticks and small pipes up into the trees, causing pecans to rain down on us. Once we collected enough pecans, we sold them to the manager of the Curb Market, a dirt floor store on East Boundary Street. He paid us the handsome sum of three dollars for a full grocery bag of pecans. This was exploitation at its finest, but this was the way things were in the south. Ultimately, all I really wanted was enough money to go downtown on Broad Street to the Imperial Theatre. The Imperial Theatre played all black movies and shows only cost ninety-nine cents each. After earning money from yard work or from selling pecans, I would ride my ten-speed bike downtown and watch movies like *Super Fly, Let's Do It Again, Shaft,* and every Pam Grier movie I could. Life was simple and good. If there was something better in life, I didn't know about it yet because the Bottom was my entire world before age fifteen.

My mother loved all three of us dearly, but to all that knew and loved her, she could be a deeply complicated, and at times, an angry young woman. Depression then alcoholism slowly crept into our lives. First cigarettes, then Smirnoff Vodka became her crutch of choice. At one point, there would be as many as three empty pint bottles in the trash when I took the trash out. If my sister and I arrived home from school on a Friday and heard Mahalia Jackson's music blaring, we knew mom was in a melancholic mood, and she was drinking. That night and the weekend would be filled with cursing and raising hell about a whole host of things. We would try to stay out of her way, but sometimes it was better for us to spend the weekend with our grandparents. My mother tried to stop drinking during this period, but tragically, when she did, she began to have grand mal seizures. On more than one occasion, my sister and I watched helplessly as our mother fell to the floor convulsing uncontrollably. This was a terrifying sight for any child.

I can remember us frantically looking for things to place in our mother's mouth to prevent her from chewing her tongue. I will never forget how vulnerable and helpless my mother looked after the seizures. She was prescribed seizure medication and the seizures stopped, but she continued to drink. Alcohol was certainly not the full story, but it certainly garnered much of the credit for most of the chaos that converged on our family. An uncle once described life on 12th Street, where he and my mother grew up, like this: "We had food in our bellies and clothes on our backs, but little to no one-on-one affection. There was little time for that." Perhaps this was because my grandmother was overwhelmed by the challenges of raising ten children. He said my grandfather didn't allow my grandmother to work outside the home. She raised the children, and he worked day and night to support the family. Perhaps my mother had resentment toward my father, other men in her life, or the difficulty of being a single mother in general. My mother was in pain. She was crying out for help but no one knew how to help her. Another uncle suggested that my mother may have seen things that haunted her, things that she couldn't come to terms with. No one in our family has been able to explain it, but I always knew she was hiding something. Unfortunately, drinking led to her lashing out in ways that often had long-term consequences for her and for us.

My father would call periodically, always making grandiose, empty promises about making things better for us. For years, I believed him. I really believed that he was going to rescue us and help my mother raise us. But none of my father's promises came to fruition. This would upset her to no end, and like many single mothers, she would say, "You're just like your damn daddy," projecting his sins onto me. It didn't help that I, like many sons (and daughters), defended him even though he wasn't supporting the family financially or emotionally. After all, this was a man who had a degree in microbiology and worked as a medical lab technologist in Washington, D.C. My father had a middle-class lifestyle, yet we were living in the Delta Manor Housing Projects receiving welfare benefits and food stamps. This was problematic on many levels, but as a child, you want to believe what your parents tell you. You still want your father to be your hero, whether he deserves such praise or not, and I believed in him and defended him for many years.

My grandparents and aunts were a supportive network, but we could tell that my mother was still very unhappy and depressed. At least once a month, my sister and I would be put out of the house in the middle of the night. My grandmother would open the door for us and simply say, "Go get in bed." Unfortunately, this was a routine that would be repeated many times. We were fortunate that we lived so close to our grandparents, and we had other family members living within walking distance of where we lived. The events of one particular morning were set in motion years before I was even born. The details of the moments leading up to the incident are vague, but my sister later told me that she and my mother were in the kitchen preparing breakfast, and my mother was cutting bacon with a steak knife. I looked forward to watching cartoons on Saturday mornings like most kids.

The Super Friends were my favorite Saturday morning cartoon, and I was sitting in the living room watching television with my back toward the kitchen. My sister said that my mother was telling me to do something, and she thought that I was ignoring her. I'll admit that I was guilty of sometimes tuning my mother out, usually during her drinking binges. This wasn't right but it was my coping mechanism. It was my way of saying this is insane. But I didn't hear my mother tell me to do anything this time. I heard her entering the room to the left of me. "You don't think I will ..." and seconds later, I felt a sharp object being plunged into my left side. My mother had just stabbed me with the sharp steak knife she was using in the kitchen. She could become very animated when she drank, but I never imagined that she would do anything to harm me or my siblings. I fell to the floor in excruciating pain, bleeding, and struggling to breathe. My left lung was punctured and air was entering the space between my ribs and my left lung, which caused my left lung to collapse. I was certain that I was dying, and began to pray The Lord's Prayer: "Our Father, who art in heaven, hallowed be thy name, thy kingdom come."

According to my sister, my mother was as shocked as she was about what she had just done. My sister ran as fast as she could to my grandparents' house to get my grandfather. Minutes later, I saw my grandfather standing over me. I don't remember what he was saying, but I grabbed his pants leg as I struggled to breath. Soon after that, emergency medical technicians entered the apartment and began to render aid, including giving me oxygen. A sacred trust had just been shattered. The unthinkable was committed by my mother, not by a stranger, not by a criminal, but by the most trusted human being on the planet. If my mother could do such a thing to me, who could I trust? A mother is supposed to be the last person to ever forsake a child no matter what. She had always been there for us despite her challenges, and she had always protected and cared for us. She always made a way. This was truly uncharted territory, even for our family, and we had seen quite a bit. I was the youngest of my mother's three children—her baby, yet I was fighting for my life on the cold, hard, concrete floor of our Delta Manor apartment.

I was rushed to University Hospital by ambulance where doctors worked frantically to stabilize me and save my life. They asked me questions as they cut my shirt off, but it was all I could do to just breath. I could not speak. The attending physician made an incision about ten inches under the stab wound, then a long clear tube was inserted into my left lung. It was sutured in place and became a part of me for several days while I was in the intensive care unit. I was thirteen years old and still in shock, confused, and traumatized by the past several hours. I felt like I was completely on my own in this sterile, cold environment bathed by bright lights, attached to tubes, surrounded by beeping monitors, and an army of nurses and doctors. My father had been missing in action since we left six years earlier, and now my mother's fate was uncertain. I thought ...

Was this my fault?

Where was my mother?

What was she going through?

Was she afraid, was she remorseful?

Everyone knew leading up to this event that something had to give. Perhaps this was God's way of getting my mother's attention and throwing all of us a lifeline, a much-needed intervention. As shocking as the news of my situation was, I don't think there were many in my family that were surprised. It is a very difficult thing to watch loved ones teetering on the brink of disaster and not be able to help them, especially when children are involved. The CPS caseworker I met at the conference visited me at the hospital, but I vaguely remember speaking with her at the time. She was primarily involved with my mother and my grandparents while I was hospitalized. She was overseeing the important matters of custody for my sister and me. There were many that empathized with us and encouraged us when my mother wasn't at her best, and I wondered if my father was going to call or visit me or would he now help us.

Even before this untimely hospital stay, I was a very restless sleeper, tossing and turning most of the night. Just after falling asleep, I rolled to my right so hard that it felt like I had pulled the tube out of my chest. I had forgotten that I was in a hospital bed attached to a machine and tube that was sewn into my left lung. The pain confirmed that I wasn't dreaming, so I quickly got used to sleeping on my back as still as possible. I had no knowledge of what was going on outside of the hospital in the first days. I wondered what was happening to my mother, how my sister was doing, and what my big brother was thinking. Soon family members began to visit me and this raised my spirits. This greatly assisted me with my recovery. Eventually, some encouraged me to say that I didn't want my mother to go to prison. And indeed I didn't. For the first time in my entire childhood I feared my mother, but I wasn't angry at her. I was just confused. Intuitively, I knew that things would never be the same between us after this incident, and we would never be a family in the same way we were after this day. At least this is what I thought in the days following, but God had another plan for both of us.

After two days in ICU, I was moved to a regular room. Initially, I had a private room, but after a day or so, I got a roommate. My roommate was an African American male about my age, thirteen or fourteen. His name was Maurice. He was from Waynesboro, Georgia, about twenty miles outside of Augusta. I was recovering from a stab wound to my left lung, and Maurice had been shot with a 12-gauge shotgun and was splattered with Birdshot pellets. His left arm was in a cast because the shotgun blast broke bones in his arm. We called ourselves the dynamic duo, and we would soon be the talk of our floor and the hospital. When my roommate's doctors came to update him on his condition, they held up his x-rays, revealing what appeared to be hundreds of pellets splattered throughout his torso. We were both very lucky to be alive, but I think he was luckier than I was having survived a shotgun blast.

We were good for each other, because we were able to distract each other momentarily and return to being teenage boys. We had both survived near fatal injuries, and at least on the surface, we both appeared to be coping well and on the mend. My physician informed me that I would probably never be able to play football or participate in track and field as a result of my lung injury. All of the men in my family participated in sports, so I heard him, but I rejected his dire prediction as soon as he made it. Before the incident, I was super skinny and on a mission to reach 110 pounds before the start of junior high school. I devoured every potato and peanut butter sandwich I could find. *I have to get better and get ready for football tryouts in the fall,* I thought. Maurice never told me who shot him nor did he discuss the circumstances that caused him to be shot. And I didn't say who stabbed me in Delta Manor nor did I divulge the details that led to my injuries. It wasn't important now, because we would have plenty of time to deal with those painful details soon enough. We talked until late each night, and we occasionally shared a painful laugh.

At one point, I almost forgot why I was at University Hospital, and I was still waiting to wake up from this elaborate dream. The doctors, nurses, and respiratory therapists were great, in fact, everyone that entered the room had impeccable bedside manners. I guess they figured we both needed a break and a little more TLC. As the days passed, I dreaded the thought of leaving the hospital, afraid of the uncertainty that awaited me outside of the hospital walls. Life and the realities ahead were on pause for a moment, but I knew the play button would be pressed again as soon as they wheeled me to the curb and helped me into my grandparents' car. I knew my sister was in good hands, but I was still worried about my mother, where she was and how she was coping. The question of where my sister and I would live was still up in the air, and I began to worry about the whispers and how I would face the many questions that neighborhood kids would have. Kids could be cruel, and I imagined the distasteful jokes and teasing I would encounter when I returned to my neighborhood in the Bottom.

It is said that you can't truly understand some things until you've walked that walk. There wasn't a soul that could help me with this, no one to provide advice, no therapist or road map leading from this place. I had to grow up really fast and decide whether I would allow this thing to destroy me, or I could use this painful episode to make me stronger. There was much I didn't know, and it was clear I would need all the help I could get going forward. And my family would be there to help me. I have often wondered how well my roommate, Maurice, recovered—both physically and emotionally from his injuries, and how well he fared over the past four decades. We didn't stay in touch, but I wish we had. For years I have wondered about what my life could have been like given my life experiences. *Why didn't I end up in a juvenile detention center, in a gang, addicted to drugs or alcohol, homeless and broken instead of being resilient and successful?* Resilience is the process of recovering from adversity due to a stressful or trauma-causing event (Seery 2010). Some people develop a psychological immunity to adversity-trauma causing events over time. Children living in a war zone, or in neighborhoods plagued by frequent gunfire and exposure to shooting victims are such examples. The near-death flag pole accident, the stabbing at thirteen, and other life-threatening scenarios had the effect of toughening me over time. Those with high levels of resiliency tend to be better prepared to handle adversity. (Dienstbier 1992)

The stabbing was severe, but my mother had never harmed me before this incident outside of corporal punishment using a belt or an extension cord. Again, reactions to abuse vary widely, and in my case, it was a mild reaction. I was one of those fortunate people that could bounce back from anything, seemingly unscathed. My nurturing support network was also integral to this resilient spirit. *One through seventeen is controlled by people and circumstances beyond my control, but seventeen and beyond is completely up to me.* This was my mantra, my internal affirmation and motivational speech to myself. Any predictions that were not positive would be used as motivation to work harder, no matter how many times I stumbled or fell.

He healeth the broken in heart,
and bindeth up their wounds.
—Psalm 147:3

THE POWER OF FAITH

O
UR FAMILY HAS attended Thankful Baptist Church for four
generations, and it has been an integral part of our family for over
ninety years. We were all baptized, regularly attended Sunday school,
and the 11:00 a.m. service throughout my childhood. From the youth choir
to vacation Bible school, my siblings and I were there. I looked forward to
hearing the gospel choir sing under the direction of Mrs. Henley and listening
to solos by Mrs. Doris Isom, Mrs. Eleanor Johnson, and Ms. Doretha Hollins.
As a child, I can even remember listening to the Reverend Jesse Jackson
speak at Thankful. Thankful Baptist Church was founded in 1840 and was
once attended by slaves. It's one of the oldest African American churches in
the country. Luminaries like Dr. W. E. B. Dubois once spoke at Thankful
and during the height of the civil rights movement, our church played a role
in organizing nonviolent protests for racial equality. Slavery and Jim Crow
made it dangerous for blacks to express their feelings years ago, and for this
reason, they took their painful secrets and problems to the grave with them
or they shared them with their pastor. The Reverend N.T. Young was a gifted
preacher, a Morehouse man, and he served as pastor for forty years. He visited

me in those first days after leaving ICU, and once again when I was released to my grandparents' custody. He knew every member of his congregation and regularly visited them when they were hospitalized. I remember Reverend Young praying with me (and for me), for my physical as well as emotional and spiritual recovery. That was all I had and it was apparently all I needed.

My strong faith had gotten me this far, and I prayed for the strength to continue. More important, I prayed for my mother and my family's healing. I prayed for the courage that would be needed as I returned to school and attempted to resume my life. My strong faith would get me through this crisis and sustain me through the many challenges that were ahead. I prayed for God to show me the way to move forward from this dark chapter in my life and to help me write a new narrative with a better ending than some predicted for me, my siblings, and my mother. I desperately wanted to prove all the naysayers wrong, and I would. This difficult chapter in my life galvanized my determination to survive and be successful. Whenever I encountered difficult people or obstacles, I would reflect on the strength that helped me survive my childhood.

My sister and I would stay with my grandparents for the remaining two years of her high school years and the next four of mine. My grandparents' home had always been a gathering place for our entire family. I am eternally grateful for their love and unconditional support throughout my childhood. African American grandmothers continue to be the irreplaceable lifeline for untold numbers of children whose parents are either unable or unwilling to love and nurture them. I never knew what was said, but whatever my mother told the police would keep her from going to prison. There were limits to her access to us, and I was okay with that. I feared her for the first time in my life, despite her challenges with alcoholism. I loved her, but I needed help moving forward from this. My strong faith and my extended family, which included community organizations, were also contributing factors. They held me up and sustained me during some of the most difficult times of my childhood, and my grandfather and uncles served as father figures in my father's absence.

My praying, loving aunts all played important roles as well. Aunt Evelyn was especially supportive over the years. She was always able to offer me sage advice and support when my mother couldn't. She became my indispensable backup mother. She was always eager to listen, offer support, and willing to offer balanced feedback. If she thought I needed a stern correction, she gave it to me followed by her saying, "Now that's that!" This meant it was over, that she never had to repeat herself. During one of my frequent visits several years ago, my aunt Evelyn's husband, Uncle Wallace said, "Boy, you sure love your Aunt Evelyn." My response was quick and from the heart. "She loved me first, Uncle Wallace." There was no social media or internet at this time, but the news of the tragedy quickly spread throughout the Bottom. Returning to school, church, and the neighborhood was very difficult for me. I believed the entire world knew what happened on that fateful Saturday morning on East Hale Street. Of course they didn't, but I carried a shame and fear of judgement and stigmatization with me for many years. In the back of my mind, despite the love I received from my village, I felt enormous pressure to prove wrong those who predicted another path for my future. It was hard enough being a poor black male teenager, but this thing made me feel like I had to be damn near perfect.

Strangely enough, I felt as if I had to apologize for things my mother did early on. My mother could be very loving at times, but she also had a way of burning bridges with folks (too often this included her siblings). When they would vent about something she said or did, it often felt like it was being directed our way, but of course, it wasn't intended to. My mother was very frustrated in the months following the incident. She had to move out of the area, and she didn't have any of her children. My mother was angry because my grandparents had custody of my sister and me, and she did everything she could to annoy them. Unfortunately, she took her frustration out on my grandparents in very creative and mean-spirited ways. One night, about three months after the incident, my mother called 911 and sent the fire and police department to my grandparents' home. It was about 2:00 a.m. and everyone in the house was awakened by flashing lights and the squelch of police radios through our bedroom windows. Of course, this woke up everyone in the neighborhood because it appeared that there was something big going on at my grandparents' home. My grandmother answered the door, angry at what she saw. There were fire trucks, an ambulance, and police cars packed in the circle out front. I can only imagine what my mother told the 911 operator that night, but whatever it was, it was convincing as hell. To say my grandmother was upset was an understatement. I can't imagine what my grandparents were going through. It was nothing short of a nightmare scenario for them.

They had raised ten children during The Great Depression, raised my older brother (who had already graduated from high school by this time), and were now raising my sister and me. And this is how my mother was repaying them. This made me want to grow up as quickly as possible and escape the rip tides that my mother created for us. I looked forward to turning the page and living a life devoid of alcoholism or dysfunction, but for now, I had to be patient and wait my turn. I was a child, helpless to control my own destiny for now. "Come here, boy!" my grandmother called out to me. I ran to the door as quickly as I could. "Yes, ma'am?" When I reached the front door, I was amazed at the spectacle that was assembled out in front of the house. It looked like someone had called in a bomb threat at a busy shopping mall. Just as I arrived, my grandmother began to tell the police officer that my mother drinks too much, and she has a history of doing crazy things when she drinks. My grandmother wanted to show the officers how unpredictable my mother could be when she drank and lashed out against her and others.

Suddenly, without warning, my grandmother pulled up my T-shirt, exposing the stab wound and my surgical scar. "See, this is how crazy his mother is," she said. "This is what she did to this boy." That graphic demonstration was more traumatic and painful than the actual stabbing was months earlier in our tiny living room. My grandmother never knew how much she hurt me with that "show and tell." I wasn't angry at her, because she was frustrated and angry at my mother, yet still, it crushed me and retraumatized me all over again. I cried myself to sleep after everything settled down and everyone left. For many years, I could be standing in the mirror with my shirt off, and I couldn't see the scars. I willed them to disappear. I willed the hurt to disappear as well. No one in my family ever discussed the events of that Saturday morning with me, and I didn't discuss it with anyone for decades, not even my wife or siblings. It was buried, or so I thought. But in 2012 while talking to a mental health colleague in Temecula, California, we stumbled upon the topic of my childhood, and I described myself as *damaged goods*.

And over the years, I would tell people that *I'm not even supposed to be here*. I was alluding to the multiple traumas, disappointments, betrayals, and discrimination I had endured since I was thirteen years old. Of course, this mortified my colleague, which prompted additional probing about the topic. The conversation opened a floodgate of raw emotions that I wouldn't see again until I met my CPS caseworker in San Diego. Where I grew up, there was a belief that if you didn't talk about it, it would just go away. I knew better, because by this time, I had a master's degree in mental health. Truth be told, I was drawn to the field of clinical social work because I was soul searching and seeking answers about myself and my family. I had a lot of stuff I was curious about, spanning decades and careers that included law enforcement and the military. To say I had seen a lot was an understatement.

Have enough courage to trust love one more
time and always one more time.
—Maya Angelou

GETTING REACQUAINTED

ONE SUNDAY AFTERNOON about six months after the incident, my grandmother and I were sitting at the kitchen table talking when she said something that would motivate me to reach out to my mother. "How can you love me if you don't care anything about your mother?" I thought this was very unfair at the time, but I thank her to this day for saying it, because it was the impetus for us to rebuild our relationship. "I do love her, and I love you too," I said. There was no way that I was going to say that it was unfair or "I'm not doing that." I agreed to go visit my mother soon, and within the week, I went to visit her at her new apartment on the Hill. She spent the rest of her days living in the Hill section of Augusta in a self-imposed exile.

My grandmother loved both of us, and she was understandably concerned about my mother, given everything that had happened. Her motherly instincts told her that she had to help both of us, and she understood that no matter how troubled my mother may have been, she and I needed to have some type of relationship. I wasn't forced to reach out to my mother, but I was voluntold to. Some still find it inconceivable that my mother and I could have such a close, loving relationship after such a traumatic event. The short answer is, my grandmother deserves the credit along with a lot of prayers for both of us. The very first one-on-one meeting was cordial but initially awkward for both of us. I could tell my mother was as nervous as I was, but she was happy that we were together again. This was an important first step, the first of many more important visits over the next several months, eventually leading to weekend stays.

We didn't have mediators or therapists, it was just the two of us. But such a meeting would have been brokered with the assistance of a clinically-trained therapist if it had happened today. Mom and I never discussed the incident, and in retrospect, this should've been the first order of business. It was an ever-present elephant in the room for decades, but we never discussed it. The closest we ever came was when she told someone an inaccurate account of what happened. When it was repeated to me, I told my mother that if she ever told anyone that lie again, she would never see me again. I always wanted her to say that she was sorry for all she had put us through, and to apologize for hurting me, but life went on anyway. I loved her, missed her, and we moved forward. My mother continued to drink, but she was very cautious in her dealings with me from that point on. Later, when I thought she was being mean-spirited toward her sisters or other family members, I would simply say, "Mom, I don't agree with that." She would listen but others didn't have it so easy. Even though my mother and I were rebuilding our relationship, my sister and I remained with our grandparents until we graduated from high school. She was still my mother, and I respected her as such, but by the time I graduated, our roles were changing.

During an assembly at my junior high school, the superintendent of schools informed us that A. R. Johnson Junior High School would become Georgia's first health professions high school starting at the beginning of the 1980 school year. I listened intently as he explained the concept of this new school, a school focused on preparing students for health professions. *I want to be a part of this, I have to attend this new school,* I thought to myself. Prior to this time, I couldn't remember being engaged in classes or being motivated to make good grades. At the time, my GPA was 2.5, and I had a good disciplinary record, which were the two major requirements. This was all that was required to apply for the inaugural class of 1980. I rushed home and asked my sister to help me write an essay so I could apply for this school. She did, and in the fall of 1980, I became one of first one hundred twenty-five students to attend the A. R. Johnson Health Professions High School.

I was super excited at the prospect of being among the first students in the state of Georgia to attend such a school. "I don't know why you're going to that school," I was warned by one of my elders. "You're not going to make it." I brushed this aside and looked forward to the start of the fall semester. I was going to attend ARJ, and I was determined to be in the first graduating class in 1983. In the first year, the school only had tenth grade and with each year that followed, the school grew by one grade. Half of the student body came from middle-class and affluent sections of Augusta. Several of my classmates' parents were physicians, some had two parents that were physicians, and others were pharmacists, professors, or educators. The other half came from South Augusta, from military families, and the rest were from the Bottom. This was the first time I attended a school that wasn't one hundred percent black.

The magnet school didn't have sports, and the curriculum was heavily focused on science and the health professions. There was no football, baseball, or track and field, which I missed. I had to settle for playing ping pong during lunch breaks. We wore white lab coats, white pants, white shoes, and we had our own stethoscopes. We even drew blood from each other in phlebotomy class starting in the tenth grade. In addition to the health/science curriculum, we were able to take part in innovative practicums, which included visiting the Medical College of Georgia that was only four blocks away. We observed human dissections, shadowed health department inspectors during restaurant inspections, and medical lab technologists doing blood and urine testing; made rounds with respiratory therapists, physical therapists, occupational therapists and other allied health professionals.

Some of our instructors were nurses and medical lab technologists. Mrs. Lavender, our biology teacher, was no nonsense and kept every class interesting and engaging. She was my favorite. "Now, now, Isaac," she would say whenever I got distracted. Ms. Smith was also popular. She was a medical lab technologist like my father, and all of our teachers were on top of their game. At one point, I was sure that I wanted to be a respiratory therapist, but I knew that my educational renaissance was still a work-in-progress. Still, I persevered and kept my grades up. During this same time, I was also attending the Upward Bound Program at Paine College across the street from Medical College of Georgia. Ms. Ernestine Harris was the director of the program, and she ran a tight ship. I really appreciate her for holding my feet to the fire during those three years. The program offered tutoring during the weekdays (and some weekends), and it paid a stipend. During the summers, we stayed on Paine College's campus, took classes, and continued to get tutoring and college preparation.

After graduating, we were able to take college courses that could be transferred to our chosen colleges in the fall. My sister and several cousins also took part in the program. During the three years I was in Upward Bound, we took wonderful, educational trips to the 1980 World's Fair in Knoxville, to Gatlinburg, Tennessee, where we visited Ruby Falls; the World Trade Center and Empire State Building in New York City, and in Washington, D.C., we visited iconic monuments and visited the U.S. Mint. During this trip, my sister and I had the chance to see our father and other D.C. family members for the first time in years. My paternal grandmother, "Granny," gathered everyone at the hotel where we were staying for an impromptu family reunion. This was the first time I had seen them since I was seven. During the eight years since we had left, my father visited Augusta twice and he called sporadically, but we had no contact with my paternal grandmother or other relatives in the area during this time. His absence essentially cut us off from them.

Years later, my father's siblings and my cousins would relay the stories about how remarkable a woman my paternal grandmother was. Sadly, by the time I began to visit D.C. as an adult, my grandmother had become gravely ill, and she passed away at the age of ninety-two in 1997. The Paine College Upward Bound Program played an integral role in my teenage years and later success. Even though I didn't initially stay in college, I learned valuable life lessons that would prove very valuable in the coming decades. It was yet another extension of my evolving, affirming village. One that would help guide me through several careers and higher education, and inspire me to one day work in higher education and model what I saw in the Paine College Upward Bound Program.

There are some things which cannot be learned quickly, and time,
which is all we have, must be paid heavily for their acquiring.
—Ernest Hemingway

DO-OVER

"**E**VERYTHING IN LIFE is not a do-over." This is what I preach to my sons and the young people I mentor to this day. It's important to make the best of every opportunity the first time, because you may not get another opportunity, and if you do get another shot, it may come at a much higher cost the second time around. This is a very hard lesson I learned after graduating from high school. After three years, I arrived at Georgia Southern College in the fall of 1984. There was absolutely no reason why I shouldn't have graduated from college in four years. My roommate was my best friend from A. R. Johnson, and he was the school's first valedictorian. I started off well enough, but I quickly lost my focus, succumbing to the sights and sounds of freedom and college life.

I had dreamed of going off to college and creating a successful life, a life far away from Delta Manor Housing Projects, but something was missing. My roommate was brilliant, and he was laser-focused on his studies as I had always known him to be, but my mind was somewhere else. I needed an encouraging voice. I needed a parent to say, "I believe in you, stay the course." I always knew that education was the great equalizer and was key to the life I dreamed of as a child growing up in the Bottom. Despite knowing better, I didn't apply myself as I should have, and I found myself sleeping in the girl's dorm more than I did my own for most of the first semester. I also drank too much, so much that my roommate began to distance himself from me. He could tell that I was blowing it, but he left me to my own devices. I don't blame him, he didn't forget why he was there. I did. He moved out after the first semester. I was falling into a self-fulfilling prophecy that predicts that children from homes with alcoholism or drug addiction are four times as likely to become substance abusers themselves. I was numbing my own pain for the first time, but I needed to find a healthier way of doing it before it was too late.

I called my grandparents and my mother, but my family back in Augusta had no idea that I was in so much pain. My aunt Jessica from D.C. called to check on me from time to time and mailed me pocket change, but she had no idea what I was going through. She would be the first from my father's side of the family to reach out and reconnect, and I owed her better. I would occasionally bum rides from Statesboro to Atlanta to see my sister, who was attending Clark College at the time. My sister was always upbeat, always had a beautiful smile, and she appeared to be unscathed by adversity. But underneath that well-honed façade, I knew she was struggling as well, yet she soldiered on, becoming the first of my mother's children to graduate from college. I am so proud of the woman, wife, mother and grandmother she became. She is an extraordinary woman, my heroine. My brother also honed successful careers in the military, advertising and newspaper industry, sales consulting, and as the owner of a successful advertising business. I am equally as proud of him.

At the start of the spring semester, I met a beautiful senior by the name of Winnie. She was also from Augusta. She had a car and she let me ride home with her occasionally. When Winnie and I started dating, I calmed down quite a bit. She was a loving, nurturing source of support, just what I needed. Little did I know that by underperforming my freshman year of college, I was losing a golden opportunity, the only opportunity I would have for a long time to just focus on college. My first semester at Georgia Southern was partially about immaturity and partly a cry for help. Afterall, I had gotten through the past four years without any lasting issues. I graduated from high school at seventeen, and my grandparents ensured that I stayed out of trouble, so everyone thought I was doing fine.

Years later, I wondered how things would've been had I attended an HBCU, if that nurturing environment would've made a difference. I think it would've. Though I had an educational renaissance from my last year of junior high school to my first year at ARJ, I still struggled with math. Instead of offering tutoring or encouragement, my male GSC math professor declared, "Everyone isn't college material, perhaps you should do something else." One day I slept in and missed English class. I was awakened by a knock on my dorm room door, and when I answered it, there stood my English professor. I was shocked.

"Can I come in?"

"Of course," I said as I invited her in and we sat on my bed. She told me that she was concerned about me, that I was doing well in her class, but I had missed three days. And then she asked a question that few had asked me since I was thirteen years old. "Are you okay?" As kind and concerned as she was, I was decades away from sharing my inner thoughts and feelings, especially about the true source of my pain. I was a master at masking my true feelings, a defense mechanism I had honed early in my childhood that proved very useful, so I thought. It was a very simple question, but I was blown away that a white professor cared enough about me and my success at GSC to track me down. My supportive village was my lifeline, but few within this network realized that I was still hurting and still in need of reassurance. I told her that I would return to class and I did. I stopped drinking and finished out the year more focused and earned a B in her class. I thanked her for her genuine concern, but I was still missing something.

One evening about a month before the end of the semester, Winnie wanted to talk with me about our future. She told me that she was graduating in a few months and was ready for the next phase of her life. She could see that I needed to get myself together and it might take a minute—more than she could give me—and she needed more than I could provide her as a broke, wild freshmen. Sadly, both assumptions were right. Winnie broke up with me and broke my heart. I lost her to a solider her age that had his stuff together. I heard that she married him a year or so after graduation. This was a wake up call for me and was one of the factors that contributed to me deciding to take a break from school and join the Marine Corps. I believed the Marine Corps could help me become more focused, more disciplined, and I wouldn't be so broke while attending school. I finished the school year with an unremarkable 2.2 GPA, and I left GSC for good in May. This was one of the biggest regrets of my life. It's never too late to go back to school or regroup in general, but my lack of focus cost me years of hardship and struggle. It would take me twenty years to complete my bachelor's degree, once I started juggling careers and a family. My best friend graduated with honors in four years, was accepted to the Medical College of Georgia, and he became a medical doctor. I would attend his graduation from medical school eight years later.

By twenty years old, I was essentially my mother's guardian. She even lived with me for a period. I was the go-to when she needed anything, especially when problem solving was required. I was the old spirit, and I could get her to do more than anyone on the planet could. She still needed a lot of looking after, even when I left Augusta for college and the Marine Corps. We spoke every weekend, and I sent her postcards and letters from everywhere I traveled. I bought her flowers, candy, clothes—anything she needed. No one would have ever imagined the past we shared based on the close bond we had. Mom knew that I would give her anything she needed, but she knew I wasn't the one to ask for alcohol and that I wasn't going to knowingly contribute to her slow destruction. She never took any AA or 12-step programs seriously, but she was prescribed Disulfiram (Antabuse), a drug prescribed since the 1950s, designed to change the way the body breaks down alcohol. If she took Antabuse and drank alcohol, it would cause her to become violently ill and have symptoms like a hangover. I don't know for sure, but I suspect that my mother was given an ultimatum from the courts to take this medication, and she could have asked for it, because she desperately wanted to stop drinking. My relationship and advocacy of my mother forced me to confront the real possibility that I could become her. This fear of becoming a self-fulfilling prophecy helped me to gain the focus I would need in the coming years to accomplish my goals.

People will try to tell you that all the great opportunities have been snapped up. In reality, the world changes every second, blowing new opportunities in all directions, including yours.
—Ken Hakuta

BRUTAL HONESTY

AFTER LEAVING GEORGIA Southern College, I found a job opening in the classifieds for a warehouse worker at Green's Frozen Foods, a food packaging company located near the farmer's market on Gwinnett Street. I spoke to the owner of the company on a Monday at about 9:00 a.m. He thanked me for coming by and told me to check back with him three days later. I agreed and returned on Wednesday of that same week and asked if there were any openings yet.

"Not yet, check back with me on this Friday, and I will let you know if I have anything," he said. I returned on Friday, and this time he met me out front. "Is that your shiny new car?" he asked, pointing at my yellow 1976 Toyota Corolla, which was about eight years old at the time. "Yes, it's my car," I said. "You're doing too good, son. You don't need a job."

The inescapable reality is that racism and discrimination will always exist and this country will continue to struggle with its shameful legacy of disenfranchising African Americans. The effects of discrimination, real and perceived, have significant ties to self-esteem, self-worth, and research suggests these can cause the onset of depression. From that day on, I refused to allow anyone to convince me that I wasn't worthy or that I didn't belong.

There would be many people, like this man, that believed with all their heart that I didn't belong, I didn't deserve, and I wasn't qualified. A month before school ended, I visited the Armed Forces Recruiting Center in Augusta and joined the Marine Corps delayed-entry program three months later with a plan of maturing and obtaining money to help pay for college after a year. I went home and informed my grandmother of my decision.

"Boy, you got a death wish?" she asked. "No ma'am, I will be fine," I said. "If it's not my time, nothing is going to happen to me." My brother was already serving in the United States Air Force in Japan. He was a security police officer and trained K9s to be military police dogs. He was poster card sharp with his razor-sharp creases, bloused boots, and black beret. The night before I shipped off to Parris Island, South Carolina, I called my brother for a pep talk and he provided his usual sage advice. "Are you nervous, little brother?"

"A little bit," I said.

"You're going to be just fine, you know why?"

"Why?" I asked.

"Because you don't have a choice."

It was true. We had a large loving family, but we didn't have a safety net if we failed or couldn't figure out how to make it after graduation. College wasn't a necessity in my grandparents' eyes but working certainly was. If you wanted to eat, you needed to work and figure it out. I was shipped to Parris Island on June 18, 1984 after joining three months earlier. It was a surreal experience arriving at the famed Parris Island, one of the only two places in the country where Marines are made. It was a rude awakening standing on the famous yellow footprints. This was a world away from the Bottom and Georgia Southern. The drill instructors immediately swarmed us, screaming demands and creating chaos, the likes of which none of us had ever experienced. We were kept up all night to test our ability to think under duress while fatigued.

The next morning, I was assigned to 3rd Battalion, I Company, Platoon 3080. My senior drill instructors were Staff Sergeants Waller and Suarez, and Sergeant Taylor was my third drill instructor. Marines never forget their drill instructors, even decades after leaving the Corps. Parris Island was a wake up call for me, just as I imagined it would be. It was Africa hot, humid, and barely visible creatures called sand fleas chewed upon our flesh constantly, but we were forbidden from swatting them or even scratching. Sand fleas were treated with the same reverence as animals on the endangered species list. There was little to nothing that I or any of us could do right. We ran everywhere and responded to our drill instructors yelling, "Sir, yes, sir!" when they called us by our collective new name "80!" The individual ceased to exist and a brand new awareness of the collective was introduced. If one recruit made a mistake, his fellow recruit would help him pay through incentive PT, which was another term for doing push-ups and other punishing exercises until you created puddles of sweat.

If we were in the chow hall and one recruit opened his mouth for any reason other than to eat as fast as he possibly could, everyone in the platoon was ordered to stop eating immediately and throw their food in the trash. We quickly learned to inhale our food for fear of not being able to finish the meal. To my surprise, I was in my element at Parris Island, and it was exactly what I needed. For three months, nothing else existed but what was on the training schedule. Life was fast-paced and chaotic; it was a place where I was finally beginning to gain much-needed clarity. As expected, I became a man at Parris Island. I graduated from boot camp in September 1984 and completed my initial active duty, including Military Occupational Specialty School (MOS) training at Camp Johnson in North Carolina. Unfortunately, no one from my family made it to my graduation from boot camp or MOS School. Four weeks before my eight-week training course was completed, I received news that my maternal grandmother had suffered a heart attack back home in Augusta. My family notified the Red Cross that my grandmother was gravely ill, protocol for when a military member needs to come home for a family emergency.

I was allowed to come home on emergency leave for one week. On the bus ride home from Jacksonville, North Carolina, I had time to reflect on all the wonderful things my grandmother had done for my siblings and me. How she nursed me back to health and gave me a safe place to heal following the incident. She was our guardian angel during the most difficult times of our childhood, and she managed to reunite me and my mother. My relatives packed the waiting room outside of the ICU around the clock. My loving grandmother appeared to be getting better, and after a few days she summoned me to her bedside. "I'm going to be fine, go back to North Carolina to complete your training," she said. I kissed her, told her I loved her, and headed back to North Carolina the next day after spending time with my mother. Little did I know, this would be the last time I would see my grandmother alive. I headed back to Camp Johnson and graduated from my training course a short time later. My youngest uncle picked me up from the Trailways bus station in Augusta, and during the ride to my grandparents' house, he informed me that my grandmother died hours earlier in the day. As we pulled into my grandparents' driveway, seeing the white bereavement wreath on the door made her death real.

My grandmother was the matriarch of our family and her loss was devastating to everyone. She was the glue that kept our family together and all of us owed her an enormous debt of gratitude, especially my siblings and I. We would have been lost had she and my grandfather not taken us in and raised us. She provided the love and stability we needed, especially after the incident. All three of us were adults and were doing well, and she and my grandfather had done more than their part. Her wish of seeing my mother and I reunited was accomplished, and she knew my siblings and I would do our best to look out for our mother.

My grandfather was lost after my grandmother's death, and he died less than a year later. They would be amazed at the incredible legacy they left behind, one that included the families first medical doctor, first lawyer, first engineer, energy executive, newspaper executive, vice principal, a mental health clinician, career military professionals, business leaders, entrepreneurs, union workers, career civil servants, a fashion designer, and several chefs. Other families from the Bottom produced equally impressive offspring, including a future city manager, professional football players, basketball players, PhD's, federal law enforcement officers, real estate executives, and a host of professional writers.

I completed another stint of active duty, but this time at the Marine Corps Logistics Base in Albany, Georgia. Four months before finishing my tour in Albany, I met my future wife. Gwen was a beautiful, Godiva chocolate-covered Georgia Peach born and raised in Albany. She captured my attention and heart instantly. We only dated for nine months before getting engaged, and we were married in Albany on March 28, 1986. We had a small wedding with a budget of five hundred dollars. My beautiful bride borrowed a dress that fit her like it was made for her, I rented a tux, and my best man wore his Marine Corps uniform. Family and friends from both sides of our families helped us with food preparation. I bought alcohol from my uncle's liquor store in Augusta and someone donated a beautiful multi-tiered wedding cake. Unfortunately, my mother was under the weather, and she couldn't travel for the wedding.

She would meet my new wife for the first time after we were married. My mother was territorial and gave my poor wife hell at first, but then she warmed up to her. My father was also a no-show. I was twenty years old, and I had my own family. We were kindred spirits, inseparable. Today we have two wonderful sons and a beautiful granddaughter, Azalia. By the grace of God, we have been married for thirty-three years. It has been said that "It's hard to be what you haven't seen," and it is difficult, but not impossible. I'll admit that it hasn't been easy because of our shared histories of childhood adversity, but our love is a testament to our shared resilience and determination to work through the difficult challenges that confront the black family. I'll admit that I am far from a perfect husband or father, but I have done my best given what I've seen. My strategy was simple. I attempted to emulate the positive examples I saw modeled by the men in my family and from my community. I vowed that I was going to do the opposite of what I saw from my parents regarding a whole range of things. I didn't drink for over twenty-six years following my second year of marriage, and I vowed to never subject my family to alcoholism or any other addictive behavior. I pledged that I would say things like, "I love you." "I'm proud of you." "You can do anything you set your sights on," and do the things I wish I could've seen during my childhood. I was determined to do whatever I had to do, so that my wife and sons could do whatever they wanted to do in life. Setting the example, as a black man, husband, father, grandfather, and mentor would be my charge.

No one would be allowed to define me or mine as "less than." Negotiation and leadership would replace belts and extension cords and feedback would always be balanced. I resolved to never bring disgrace upon my family or my community, and I would never abandon the people I loved. I surrounded myself with like-minded, positive thinking people and organizations that fostered growth and good will. If you're always the only person in the room affirming and encouraging, you're in the wrong room. Change it as soon as possible! Sometimes love is not enough. It's sometimes difficult for partners to recognize how important it is to have a "safe space." I would often tell my bride that I could handle the weight of the world, no matter what life threw my way, but I needed a safe, loving place to retreat to, a place to regroup, especially while serving in law enforcement, the Marine Corps, and high-pressure sales and recruiting careers.

Sometimes people can be standing right next to you: family, friends, colleagues, *but still not be able to see or hear you,* because you appear to be coping too well. This was true in my childhood and throughout my adulthood. This is not an indictment of anyone, but sometimes even loving, nurturing family and friends fail to notice when their loved ones are in pain. Perhaps this was because I became an expert at masking and soldiering through things that would have broken the average person. I regret that I haven't always shown restraint, been as artful in my communication or as patient as I could've been at times, but I tried to give my wife and my sons a better life. One I couldn't dream of when I was growing up, a life full of unlimited possibilities. The *quantity* amount of time was often a problem due to my work schedules, but I always ensured that I had *quality* time with my family. We learned to master the cheap and impromptu two-day vacations until we were able to take seven and eleven-day cruises.

My wife witnessed some of my most difficult years working in dangerous jobs, dealing with frequent travel and health concerns, high stakes politics, discrimination and adversity. She has seen me bloodied and tattered, but through it all, she has never given up on me, even when things didn't look so promising. I am eternally grateful for her love and support and that of my two sons, Davitric and Isaac III, my precious granddaughter, Azalia, and my phenomenal village of family and friends. It is my hope that by telling my story, they too will gain a greater understanding of who I am and from whence I have come. At the same time, I want to give others insight into some of the little things they can say and do to support their families, friends, and those they advocate for when they are in crisis. Sometimes just asking the question, "Are you okay," and listening could be life changing. Hearing someone say, "I see and hear you," could be the difference between life and death, or success and failure for those in need.

*The ultimate measure of a man is not where he stands
in moments of comfort and convenience, but where he
stands at times of challenge and controversy.*
—Dr. Martin Luther King Jr.

PROTECT AND SERVE

ON JANUARY 28, 1986, I was sworn in as a patrolman with the Augusta Police Department. My take home salary was less than $1,100 after taxes and deductions. I was back in the city where I grew up and embraced the job as a patrolman, working some of Augusta's most dangerous areas. Each day before going on patrol, I said a simple prayer: "Lord, let me come home alive and help me to do my best by the people I am sworn to protect." I also read the first verse of Psalms 27, "The Lord is my light and my salvation, whom shall I fear? The Lord is the stronghold of my life, of whom shall I be afraid?" It didn't take long to appreciate how difficult the job of a law enforcement officer was. I also learned that black officers had much more to worry about than just bad guys and coming home alive. It was a different era, where overt displays of intolerance and retaliation were legal.

We drove Ford Crown Victoria cruisers, wore black on black uniforms, black polished leather utility belts and black patent leather shoes. We carried 6-inch Smith & Wesson 38 revolvers, +P hollow point bullets, a mace canister, a black wooden nightstick, and metal cages separated officers from suspects in patrol cars. In the Marine Corps, every day was an inspection, so I wore my police uniform like I wore my Marine Corps uniform—with pride.

There were no cell phones or computers in our patrol cars back then, and we used cross reference books for directions because MapQuest didn't exist. On my first night on the street, I was assigned a partner, and we were dispatched to a drive-by shooting call. Upon arrival, a black female in her early twenties was found lying in the middle of the intersection near Lucy Laney High School.

Just three years earlier, I graduated from A. R. Johnson Health Professions High School, and now I was investigating shootings, stabbings, and murders, steps away from where I attended school. She was bleeding profusely from a bullet wound to her right shoulder. She initially said that an unidentified orange car drove by and someone shot her through the passenger window before speeding off. We looked for the car all night, and later she revised her story and admitted that she slapped her girlfriend out of jealousy and her girlfriend shot her in the arm. As the ambulance approached blocks away, the partner I was assigned to that night pulled out his sandwich as if nothing had happened. As insensitive as his actions seemed, it was a testament to how some people get desensitized to certain sights and sounds or difficult things over time. Life has a way of numbing us to things after a while.

My own life experiences had inoculated me to a range of things: disappointment, abandonment, discrimination, people counting me out, but I never lost my empathy. I never became numb to human suffering or injustice. If anything, my difficult life experiences made me even more compassionate, a champion for those that are undervalued and dismissed by society. I investigated burglaries, shootings, stabbings, murders, and rapes. I had knives pulled on me, a gun, and I was dispatched to bar fights to mundane routine calls. No matter how much I saw, I never got used to responding to calls involving injured or murdered women or children. Such calls kept me up at night. I can still remember the names of the youngest victims I encountered over thirty years ago. One such call involved a ten-year-old African American boy who was left alone with his one-month old little sister. His mother left him to babysit the little girl, and after trying in vain to stop her from crying, he placed a pillow over her face to quiet her not realizing the danger this presented to his little sister.

I was solo that day, the first on scene, and I attempted to revive this tiny, delicate, angel to no avail. Soon an EMS worker arrived in an extrication truck, a truck used to cut victims out of mangled cars. He was also alone. Another patrol unit arrived minutes later and took custody of the ten-year-old boy. I placed the paramedic in the back of my patrol car with the little girl, and I drove Code 3 to University Hospital as he continued to try and revive her. Despite every attempt to save the little girl, she was pronounced dead at the hospital. Her ten-year-old brother was too young to commit a crime according to Georgia Law, but I am sure it adversely affected the rest of his life. I never forgot this tragic situation, nor Petra, the little girl's name. I would soon find out just how dangerous a routine call could become.

As I entered the security office of a local grocery store on 15th Street, I was greeted by the store manager who took me to the security office where the shoplifting suspect—a well-built African American male in his early thirties—was being held.

Before I could handcuff him, he punched me in my chest with enough force to push me backward. He ran out of the store, and I chased him through the surrounding neighborhood. We jumped over fence after fence in the sweltering, Georgia heat, as startled residents looked on out of their back doors, and a few of them called 911. The dispatcher cleared the net, meaning all radio traffic ceased, and all available officers were dispatched to the area. I could hear the sirens approaching from every direction as he and I faced off, exhausted from the four-block chase. As I attempted to cuff him, he grabbed me and we fell to the ground. Within a minute of the grappling, I could feel him grabbing and dislodging my 38 revolver from my holster. Our holsters had a safety feature that was designed to secure the service revolver in place. It wasn't just a matter of making the arrest anymore. This simple shoplifting call turned into something much more menacing.

All I could think about was that my wife was due to deliver my youngest son within the month. Once again, I was in a fight for my life, and I had to see this through. After what seemed like a thirty-minute struggle, I regained control of my gun and the suspect, just minutes before responding officers arrived to assist me. Upon arrival, fellow officers asked me if I was all right, and placed the cuffed suspect in my patrol car. We were both drenched in sweat, exhausted, and bleeding, but by the grace of God, I went home that night, and I didn't have to use deadly force. There would be many more close calls over my two and a half years on the police department. I was on the evening shift, and we were dispatched to an apartment because neighbors called in a domestic disturbance. Seconds before reaching the front door, gunshots rang out. I was the first to enter the apartment and two other officers followed closely behind me. It is a very unnatural impulse running toward imminent danger, especially in the direction of gunshots, but that's what law enforcement and servicemembers do every day.

With guns drawn and my adrenaline high, we cleared the living room before entering the couple's bedroom. Upon entering the bedroom, I discovered an African American male in his early twenties, lying face up with a small caliber handgun in his hand. His eyes were open, and he had a single gunshot wound to his temple. The room was filled with the smell of gunpowder and death. I checked his pulse and confirmed that he was deceased. He died instantly. Then I turned my attention to the African American female, around the same age, who was slumped against the bedroom wall. She appeared to have an entry wound on the left side of her temple and a bulge on the right side of her head where the bullet had traveled. Her eyes were open, and she stared straight ahead at me. She made the most blood curdling sounds I had ever heard, and I felt completely helpless to assist her. An ambulance could be heard blocks away, but I knew instinctively that she was making her transition. The EMS workers soon confirmed what I thought.

There was nothing anyone could do for her except stay with her. We all watched helplessly as she took her last labored breaths over the most agonizing five minutes I ever experienced up until that point. She was someone's child and a mother, and I prayed for both of them and their families. She succumbed to her injuries in that apartment, but she didn't die alone. And while waiting for the coroner, I remembered where I had seen the deceased male before. I knew his family from junior high school.

We were on day shift, and I had a new African American officer, Officer Grady, shadowing me. He was a muslim, a New Yorker, and he was poster card sharp. Officer Grady had recently separated from the army and was only on the force for a few weeks. He was a great guy, and like me, he believed in fairness and equity in policing. We were near the area where fellow officers were pursuing a suspect, and I notified dispatch that we would be out with the call. As we exited the patrol vehicle, several white officers were wrestling with the suspect and things got out of control as is often the case. "That's not right. That's not right," Officer Grady said.

I reached into the melee and pulled the suspect out, cuffed him, and placed him in one of the officer's car. This eliminated the need for continuing the free-for-all. When we got back to our vehicle, I gave Officer Grady some on-the-job training. "You will be conflicted by the actions of some we serve with, but there are creative and resourceful ways of doing the right things." When we got to the headquarters, we were summoned to Lieutenant Furman's office, where the three white officers who were "wrestling" with the suspect were waiting for us. "Officer Grady refused to help us, and we feared for our safety," they all testified. When asked about the accuracy of their account, I spoke my truth. "That didn't happen." And Officer Grady repeated his position on the matter at hand. "That's not right." Officer Grady was fired on the spot without an investigation and without a Police Benevolent Association representative present. I was shocked, but I shouldn't have been.

It was Friday afternoon, and I was dispatched to the Department of Motor Vehicles (DMV) to investigate a report of an intoxicated middle-aged white male who was attempting to climb over the counter and assault two female DMV employees. Upon arrival, I found a very intoxicated, combative white male in his late forties cursing and he was attempting to assault the female employees. The women were terrified and feared for their safety. It was a miracle he didn't harm himself or anyone else during his drive to the DMV. Anyone that intoxicated in the middle of the day was clearly an alcoholic. I arrested him for public drunkenness and disorderly conduct. He was booked into the Richmond County Jail, and I thought that was the end of it. The next week, Lt. Furman summoned me to his office. "Go to the nearby fire station and ask to speak to Captain Garrett," he said. I asked him if there was something I was supposed to be doing at the fire station. "He will tell you what to do once you get there," he said. "You'll know what to do."

At the fire station, I asked a firefighter to direct me to Captain Garrett's office. Still in the dark, a firefighter escorted me to his office, and to my shock,

Captain Garrett was the combative, drunk customer from the DMV that I arrested four days earlier. "You owe me an apology, don't you?" he said with a big smile on his face. He was clearly proud of the privilege he had, and he wanted me to know that police leadership was on his side. In his eyes, I was "less than," illegitimate and I had forgotten my rightful place. "I arrested you for public drunkenness and disorderly conduct," I said. "No apology is required." Then I walked out of the fire station, got into my patrol car, and returned to my beat. Apparently, by arresting this individual, I had violated an unspoken good ole boy code, and now I was on someone's "list." Moral courage is a notable thing, but having it often extracts a cost. This is the way it has always been and always will be. I never ran from the consequences of doing what I thought was right as a police officer or Marine.

Since I was a child, I had a simple philosophy: *I don't expect anyone to give me anything, but you had better not try to take anything from me.* I wasn't going to jail because of anyone else's dirt, and I wasn't going to jeopardize my reputation in the community trying to cover for bad cops. I had just arrived at the station when an officer approached me as I was entering the roll call room. "Your mother is down in the lock up," he said. I knew it was retribution time, get back! I went down to the lock up and sure enough my mother had been arrested by the officers on the previous shift. Again, roles were reversed. I never had a chance to get in trouble, because I was always trying to look out for my mom.

"Mom, is this where you want to be?" She could tell I was hurt by this embarrassing situation. They released my mother on her own recognizance once I showed up.

Attempting to do the right thing quickly put me at odds with some officers and some in leadership. I was expected to write reports that reflected the prevailing consensus and not necessarily the truth. And this was problematic for me, especially because of the possible ramifications for those arrested. I always put myself and my family in the place of those I encountered on the job. I agreed to become a police officer, but I never agreed to abuse my authority, mistreat people, or lie to cover up questionable police behavior. Afterall, if that were the case, the police department didn't need diversity, inclusion, or me.

I was on the evening shift when I was assigned to work with a fellow African American officer from A-detail, someone I considered to be a friend.

He was my youngest son's godfather. We were about the same age, and we both grew up in Augusta, but we often disagreed about his aggressive tactics in black areas of the city.

"Hurry up, Ike (my nickname), I got to go lock up some niggers," he said as we loaded our car for the start of the evening shift. He and I had completely different philosophies regarding our approach to policing. I didn't consider the citizens of the Bottom to be niggers or quotas. They were my neighbors, relatives of people I knew, people we went to school with, members of my church—law abiding citizens. I took pride in my badge and job, but I wasn't prepared to sell my soul or my reputation for this or any future job. He and I had a heated conversation over those comments and came close to throwing blows. It was the weekend, so he was intent on stopping, frisking, and arresting as many black men as he could by the end of our shift to get points with Lt. Furman. Of course, he wouldn't be saying the same thing if we were assigned to a white section of the city that night. This doesn't fly in any white neighborhood in the United States. This is an unspoken and universally accepted fact that all police officers understand.

Three months earlier, following seven days on the midnight shift, I was off-duty and walking near Daniel Village Shopping Center when two white officers pulled their patrol car up next to me. They had determined that I was somehow suspicious, and they felt they had probable cause enough to stop me. The officers asked me where I was headed and where I had just came from, and I informed them that I had just left the reserve center located behind the shopping center. They asked me if I had identification, and I gave them my driver's license. After that, they began to check my pockets, apparently checking for drugs or weapons. Again, I was walking while black in a white area near my reserve center in civilian clothes. I asked them why they felt it necessary to frisk me for simply walking down the street. My car was parked at the reserve center, and I had decided to walk the short distance to the grocery store. Just before they were about to call dispatch to run my driver's license, I identified myself as Officer Ford from A-detail. They apologized profusely, saying they were sorry they didn't know I was a fellow officer. But they missed the point. They profiled me for no other reason than being a young black male in a white neighborhood.

It was for this reason that I disagreed with profiling and arbitrary "stop and frisk" sweeps. Sadly, not much has changed in the past thirty years, and in many ways, things have gotten worse regarding African American police interactions. When I rode alone, I could do police work the way I thought it should be done. But when you're assigned a partner, whatever your partner does affects you. If your partner has a good reputation in the community, that will reflect on you as his or her partner. If your partner had a reputation as a thug with a badge who violated citizens' rights, so would you. Good police officers are killed each year because of the actions of bad cops who abuse their authority and the public. While sitting in my car one Sunday afternoon, completing an incident report, I heard a loud sound that resembled a gunshot. Thankfully, it wasn't a gunshot this time, someone had thrown a brick threw the back window of the patrol car. When bad guys seek retribution, they don't bother to find individual offenders, they just look for anyone wearing the uniform, usually good officers with families.

My conscious would soon prove my undoing, but I didn't care. I had principles, and I was going to stick with them. I had just signed a petition along with eight other African American officers condemning the actions of a white Officer Blackstone for his serial use of racial slurs against members of the public and fellow officers. After signing the petition, Lt. Furman assigned me to work with Officer Blackstone, hoping he would be able to set me up. A few months later, another fellow officer from A-detail was bragging about having "screen tested" a black male he had arrested in the Bottom. Screen testing was a tactic employed by some officers when an arrestee was disrespectful or spat on them through the metal cage in the patrol cars. While the suspects hands were cuffed behind his/her back, the officer would speed up and suddenly slam on the brakes, causing the arrestee to slam their face into the metal cage, resulting in them sustaining facial injuries. I had seen my share of angry suspects and more than a few spat on me through my car's metal cage. Still, I never took part in retribution of any form. It was abundantly clear to me that I had to stay alive and stay away from internal affairs. I confronted the officer about his actions and this led to the officer speaking to Lt. Furman. "Officer Ford has a problem with police procedures," he said. Indeed, I did have a problem with what he did, and he was bragging about.

The injured man later retained legal representation and the officer had to explain how the man sustained facial lacerations while in the officer's custody. We were sworn-in as police officers with enormous discretion and power, but we weren't above the law. Life and death decisions must be made within the blink of an eye when you're on patrol, but if there was time, I negotiated with suspects, even those holding bats and knives, if there was a safe distance between us and there was no immediate threat to anyone else. Some officers are trigger-happy and can't wait to take a life. Thankfully, I was able to talk several suspects into laying down their weapons, avoiding the use of deadly force. The officer that intentionally caused the man's injuries was cleared of using excessive force, despite the man's extensive facial injuries. Chief Conner called me into his office days later with Lt. Furman in tow. Chief Conner told me that Lt. Furman informed him that he has had several issues with me over the past several months. I didn't know how to respond because I had never received a write up or a single complaint from the public. "Officer Ford, you are being terminated," Chief Conner said. I wasn't allowed to have a representative from the Police Benevolent Association present despite paying dues for over two years.

"Chief, what are the charges?" I asked.

"We have had problems with you."

"What exactly does that mean, Chief?" Chief Conner couldn't answer the question and neither could Lt. Furman. He asked for my firearm and my shield and with that I was no longer an Augusta police officer. I slowly removed my firearm, unloaded it, and placed it on the chief's desk pointing away from him along with my badge. Ironically, under this same chief of police, an officer shot and killed an African American police officer in the police roll call room the year prior. Chief Conner didn't fire him, but allowed him to resign and the officer was quickly hired as an armed security guard. The screen-testing officer also enjoyed job security along with several other officers who had received multiple complaints from the public including Officer Blackstone.

The National Black Police Association (NBPA) mission is to "Increase the awareness of the community, to be the conscience of the Criminal Justice System, and to enhance the quality of life in the African American community." This national organization of professional black law enforcement officers

(NBPA), under the leadership of Officer Ronald Howard, heard about me from my colleague, Mrs. Ophelia Adams, and officers flew in from around the country, including New York, Los Angeles, Miami, Washington, D.C., and Chicago police departments. Reverend Kenneth B. Martin, pastor of Antioch Baptist Church, graciously offered his sanctuary as a rallying point for supporters, politicians, and activists before the planned march to the Richmond County Law Enforcement Center. Dr. Joseph Lowery of the Southern Christian Leadership Conference (SCLC), State Representative Tyrone Brooks, City Councilwoman Kathleen Beasley, Reverend N. T. Young, Rev. T. O. Lampkin, and other local clergy all attended the rally before we marched to the front door of the Richmond County Law Enforcement Center.

It was a very important gesture of solidarity, having local black clergy and national luminaries on hand with local black politicians including former Mayor Ed McIntyre. I walked in the front with my wife and Mrs. Ophelia Adams, holding signs and chanting, "I will stop fighting when the truth is told!" Behind me marched dozens of African American police officers from all over the country dressed in their department's uniform. It was an awesome sight to behold police officers with the courage of their convictions willing to advocate for a fellow officer in Augusta. Chief Conner refused to even meet with NBPA leaders to discuss the circumstances surrounding my firing. The mayor was also conveniently unavailable. He and others in leadership just looked out the window at the marchers that were assembled. I am eternally grateful to Rev. Kenneth B. Martin, the late Rev. N.T. Young, Dr. Joseph Lowery, local representatives, the NBPA, and all of the officers who converged in Augusta for their encouragement, mentorship, and unwavering support.

From a young age, I learned to speak up and advocate for myself and others. I was an avid reader and consumer of history, who marveled at the courage and sacrifices our ancestors displayed in the face of death for principles and equality. I had a belief that injustice had to be met with a response, so after I marched, I used the $4,000 from my police pension to hire a lawyer, but unfortunately, local politics made it impossible for me to get due process. My family was mortified by my public fight with the Augusta Police Department, especially my mother, and several voiced concerns for my safety. After all, many of them lived through the Augusta riots of 1970 and watched as local law enforcement got away with shooting six black men, ages eighteen through thirty-nine, in the back, twenty years earlier. One of the men was shot in the back nine times and no officers were disciplined for the killings. But for me, going public was the only thing that kept me alive.

At the time, it didn't change anything, but I had to believe the issues I raised improved the plight of officers that came after me. Once the rally was over and the high profile supporters left town, it was business as usual. Months later, a manager at Damascus Woods Apartments said some very disrespectful things to my wife, and she ran to our apartment crying. I went to speak with him, man to man, and apparently I hurt his feelings, so he called the police. Officers quickly arrived on the scene in mass, and I was arrested for using fighting words. I was quickly released and the charges were dropped, but they used this incident to plaster my name in the Augusta Chronicle. Barbara Gordon, editor for the Metro County Courier, ran an article supporting me. I was blackballed from working in law enforcement and even received a stern warning from the commanding officer of my Marine Corps Reserve unit (at the time) about my "activities." Translation: he was looking for a way to bring adverse actions against me in the Marine Corps Reserves because I was fighting for my rights against the Augusta Police Department. It was surreal.

Much is said about the debt we owe to the men and women in uniform, both law enforcement and the military, and I agree one hundred percent. After all, I have worn both uniforms and taken both oaths to serve and defend. I risked my life in the service of my country and for my local municipality, and suffer with the visible and unseen wounds from that service to this day. Yet, with this awesome trust and power comes responsibility. The Augusta Police Department was merged into the Richmond County Sheriff's Department years later, when the city and county governments consolidated, and now a new sheriff is working to transform it and create a world-class department. The citizens of Augusta deserve nothing less. African Americans continue to this day to be subjected to negative evaluations in employment, by school systems, and the criminal justice system, leading to feelings of powerlessness. Strong representation in the political arena is the key to gaining fairness, equity, and social justice in these arenas.

My experiences as a police officer reinforced my determination to succeed and live my truth, even if it cost me in the short term. I truly learned what racism was during my time as a police officer, and I internalized the hurt from that experience for years. It was yet another trauma. There are those that relish the opportunity to keep you in a certain space. They attempt to define you by your race, sex, sexual orientation, religion, socio-economic status, immigration status, by where you start in life and by what happens to you. Unfortunately, some people refuse to see you through any other lens other than a negative one, one created by people and circumstances beyond your control. It's important to remind yourself that you are not defined by any of these parameters or your past. You can create a new narrative and new brand. I resolved years ago that I would reject any predictions about my life or my possibilities unless they were positive. I created the character for my life story—imperfect but confident, courageous, and unrelenting. I found my true voice when I was discharged from University Hospital.

This is what drove me during and after my time as a police officer, and during every challenge since that time. I knew I had a long way to go in my recovery, but I didn't allow anyone to dictate my path or potential since that time. I never asked anyone to give me anything in life, I simply asked for an opportunity. I never felt like I had job security no matter how hard I worked or how successful I was, and in many ways, this served me well. As in the military, failure wasn't an option. If I had a misstep or failed at anything, I had to get back up and regroup. In later years, this saved my life and helped me to persevere through several different careers and crises. I sold cars for six months at the Hyundai dealership on Washington Road. I wore crisp, creased shirts, pressed slacks, and polished black leather shoes with holes in the bottom covered by cardboard for insoles. Then, I became a licensed insurance agent and sold life, health, property and casualty insurance for a debit insurance company.

Debit insurance agents not only sold insurance, they collected insurance premiums door to door and were known to carry a lot of cash after collecting money at the first of each month. One day I let my wife ride along with me, and she watched in horror as a young man approached me just a few feet away from our car. "I ought to rob you." I stared him down and he decided against trying to rob me this day, but things could have ended very differently. Once again, I gained valuable insights and experience that would prepare me for the next challenges and opportunities ahead. I believe everything happens for a reason, though we don't always understand it at the time. I had a village in my childhood, but I never felt like I had a safety net, so I was relentless in my fight to support my family and to succeed.

Darkness cannot drive out darkness; only light can do that.
Hate cannot drive out hate; only love can do that.
—Dr. Martin Luther King Jr.

OPERATION DESERT
SHIELD AND STORM

THE FEAR OF dying, either as a cop on the beat or in a war zone, gives you a unique perspective on life. You become keenly aware of your mortality and appreciative of things that most don't. On August 1, 1990, Iraqi leader Saddam Hussein shocked the world when he brazenly invaded his oil-rich neighbor, Kuwait, prompting President George H. W. Bush to form a coalition to remove his forces. We watched CNN coverage from home as a massive buildup began in September, and in December of 1990, my Marine Corps Reserve unit was called up. This was the largest buildup of military forces since Vietnam, and as a result, Reserve and National Guard units were called at record levels. My wife and mother watched CNN nonstop, worried to death as most families were. We reported to Camp Lejeune, North Carolina within days and after another week, we deployed to Al Jubail, Saudi Arabia in January 1990.

We hit the ground just after the Christmas holidays and quickly prepared for what was billed as the "mother of all wars." The military quickly deployed hundreds of thousands of troops to the region to fight Saddam Hussein's aggression and liberate the Kuwaiti people. I was struck by the irony of being sent eight thousand miles from home to fight for Kuwaiti liberation and oil, when just months earlier, I was fired and persecuted for standing up for the citizens of Augusta. I didn't exactly feel free or liberated. I was a U.S. Marine, and I loved my country, but like many who served before me, I was conflicted. Back home, I was still "less than" in the eyes of some. The military buildup was so fast, that commercial airlines were utilized to transport troops to the war zone. Once we were in Saudi Arabia, we quickly constructed and reinforced our position with what seemed like a million sand bags. We were positioned about 100 yards from the port of Al Jubail.

A mile in the other direction, Navy and Marine Corps Aircraft were staged and made day and night sorties, bombing the hell out of Saddam's troops. We could hear the nonstop naval gunfire off in the distance as well. Saddam Hussein returned the favor by sending Scud missiles in our direction, day and night. Because of the aircraft, ships, and supplies outside of the port city of Al Jubail, a disproportionate number of Scud missiles were launched in our direction. Saddam Hussein especially enjoyed the time between 11:00 p.m. and midnight. This earned Al Jubal the nickname "Scud bowl." There were several Patriot missile batteries located within a hundred yards of where we ate and slept. The constant threat of Scud missiles hitting our position carrying chemical weapons loomed in our minds 24/7. We were trained to be able to put on our MOPP (Mission Oriented Protective Posture) gear within nine seconds of hearing air raid signals and Patriot missiles being launched. The constant fear was too much for some Marines and some imagined that they were smelling and tasting chemical agents during the nightly raids.

We were warned that the Scud missiles contained deadly nerve and blister agents, weapons Saddam Hussein used to kill thousands of Kurdish men, women, and children. On one fateful night, a Patriot missile intercepted a Scud missile headed for our position, but the falling debris landed on a tent full of reservists, killing fourteen troops as they slept. Word of this incident spread quickly and the fear of being killed by a Scud missile was front and center in all of our minds. Iraqi troops surrendered to coalition forces in waves, and President George H. W. Bush ended the war, deciding against invading Iraq. Fortunately, everyone in my unit returned from the conflict alive and in one piece, but I didn't leave the war zone unscathed. I left with PTSD, gastrointestinal problems, insomnia, and depression. Few service members return from war without being changed in some way. At the start of the war, we were ordered to take experimental medications that were intended to protect us from anthrax.

Many servicemembers were apprehensive about taking drugs that were fast-tracked by the FDA. I was among them, but we were ordered to take the medication, and told that if we didn't and we were killed in a chemical attack, our families would forfeit our Servicemembers Group Life Insurance (SGLI), which was valued at $250,000 in 1990. Saddam Hussein ordered his troops to torch the Kuwaiti oil fields as U.S. troops ran them out of Kuwait. The result was thick black billowing smoke plumes and black rain during downpours. I picked up a stomach bug that made me feel like I would die on the toilet. The mission was still front and center, and we made it happen. I competed for a meritorious sergeant board while we were in the country, and as a result, I was meritoriously promoted to sergeant in Saudi Arabia before we returned to the states. We returned to a hero's welcome from a much more appreciative public, something that was denied to fellow veterans who had fought in the Vietnam War.

As with many returning warriors, the jubilation of reuniting with your family is tempered by readjustment challenges. Families get used to not having you around, and so it takes time to get to know each other again. After the Gulf War, I remained on active duty until my official retirement date in October 2009. I was what the military calls a geo-bachelor. I bought a new home in Augusta, keeping my family in place for the next ten years. I lived in North Carolina, South Carolina, and Georgia, spending five years juggling a mortgage, rent, and utilities on the road.

I had survived and thrived in the face of tragedy and poverty, and I had survived Marine Corps boot camp. Every such slight and repressive experience further strengthened my resolve to succeed. I didn't look at failures as the end, it was simply a reminder that I needed to refine my focus on my next try.

During this time, I was blessed to lead several recruiting stations, a job I loved. I saw myself in many of the hundreds of young men and women I recruited and prepared for boot camp. Many of them were also from humble beginnings like me, single-parent homes, and most needed a big brother or a father figure. I relished this role and recognized it as an opportunity to pay forward the support I received growing up. I have remained involved in many of their lives over the past twenty-five years and followed their success. I drove home from the duty stations in the Carolinas virtually every weekend. I kept in touch with my mother by telephone during the week and made my way to the Hill to see her as soon as I got in town. If she needed anything, she knew I was there, and my wife filled in if she needed to go anywhere while I was away. My sister and brother lived out of town as well, but they both stopped in regularly and our very large extended family was on hand if mom needed anything. My mother was in very good hands in Augusta. When I got orders to the west coast, I was still there for her, but I was too far away to be able to drop what I was doing and run back to Augusta as I had done while stationed in the Carolinas between 1992-2002.

My mother and I talked every weekend, and I could tell that the drinking was beginning to take a toll on her health. For over twenty years, my siblings and I lived in constant fear of getting a telephone call informing us of something dire. In May of 2002, I was assigned to the Marine Corps Recruiters School in San Diego, California as an instructor. I trained hundreds of Marine recruiters over the next three years in public speaking, professional selling skills, and recruiting strategies. Later, I served on the General's staff as a regional trainer and trained Officer Selection Officers (OSOs) throughout the country on best-proven recruiting practices and diversity strategies. In August of 2004, we bought our second home in Temecula, California in hopes of cashing in on the white-hot housing market before it cooled off. My youngest son, his friend, and I made two round trips between San Diego and Temecula, trying to complete the move into our new home before work the next day. I was completing the last year of my three-year tour at Marine Corps Recruiters School, and I was scheduled for orders in about a year. I was discouraged by Marines that had already bought multiple homes and already cashed out, but the white-hot real estate market was too tempting to stay out of it.

Homes were increasing $20,000 in value a month. I debated before I jumped into the fray, rationalizing that I could buy and sale within the year, making a cool $100,000 profit, then head back east. Tired after a long night of driving and moving, I turned the corner to our new street, and three doors down from our home I saw a neighbor standing in his front yard. Being from the south, I instinctively stopped, rolled down my window and introduced myself. "My name is Isaac and my family and I moved in last night," I said as I extended my hand out my passenger side window. "We have a nice neighborhood," he said without hesitation. "We don't have any problems, and we want to keep it that way." I learned to recognize when bigoted people were trying to draw me into situations that could lead to adverse outcomes. In other words, scenarios that could cause me to lose everything I spent a lifetime building: my education, experience, reputation, and my ability to support myself and my family. Some predicted failure years ago, because of factors I was helpless to control. I refused to validate the stereotypes he had about me, my race, or my family. Been here before and I knew it wouldn't be the last time. I had to remind myself that I was in sunny, liberal, yet open-minded California, a beautiful state I had come to love because of its diversity.

I rolled up my window without uttering a word and proceeded to my garage, two doors down. I pulled into the garage, let the door down behind me, and shared the experience with my wife. I guess I hadn't done enough in his eyes to demonstrate me being fit enough to be his neighbor. Bigotry seemed to be an inescapable fact of life. Fortunately, we soon met other more hospitable neighbors that were much more welcoming. They have been wonderful over the years. Still, this didn't stop others from egging the front of our new home and car, costing me thousands of dollars. In the Bottom, everyone spoke to each other and were cordial, but even in a neighborhood where the cheapest home cost $400,000, he considered my family to be "less than." We didn't belong.

In the Bottom, we all coexisted: white collar, blue collar, GEDs and PhDs. Neighbors would even cut each other's grass if needed. I made time to attend a monthly neighborhood association meeting where I stood up and introduced myself and my family. I told them to feel free to stop by and chat, because when people know more about each other, they are less likely to fear each other and perpetuate stereotypes. We remained the only African Americans on our street for the next ten years, and one of two African American families within five blocks of our subdivision for over eight years. I love Southern California's weather, and for the most part, it is a more progressive, accepting state. Still, at times, I call it "Calibama," because some of the things I have encountered remind me of deep south sensibilities. Again, after a lot of hard work and sacrifice, I was absorbing yet another jab, like charcoal absorbing impurities from your stomach and liver.

With years of recruiting and leadership experience, I had planned to work in sales or recruiting after retirement. Originally, I had planned to remain on active duty for thirty years, but as fate would have it, my beautiful bride became ill. She had two seizures over an eighteen-month period, and as a result, she couldn't drive for six months following the first, and a year after the second. With no other family located on the west coast to drive her to medical appointments and both sons serving on active duty in the Air Force (one was on his third deployment to Iraq and the other was in Abilene, Texas), I was forced to either retire at twenty-five years or leave my wife stranded without support due to orders. When an active duty family member is undergoing medical care for such situations and adequate facilities and resources are available, as was the case with San Diego, the family member is placed on the Exceptional Family Member Program (EFM).

They remain in place along with the military sponsor until the evaluation or crisis is over. This program allows for continuity of care for the family member and ensures that the servicemember is on hand to support their dependent. San Diego has the second largest military population in the country (second only to the D.C., Maryland, and Virginia area) with eight military bases, three of which were Marine Corps installations. Balboa Naval Medical Center and UCSD Medical Center were also here in San Diego with the best medical specialists available to treat my wife. The Marine Corps Recruiting Command gave me orders despite my wife's condition, which meant I was going to have to report to another assignment out of state within a month. I made the only choice I could make and refused the orders, which meant I had to retire immediately. I apologized to my wife on behalf of the Marine Corps for not being more empathetic given our family's situation, but I told her we would be fine. I couldn't remember not being a Marine. I had what was considered "broken time," which meant I served in the reserves and active duty, so leaving active duty at that time essentially meant I was forfeiting a significant amount of retirement income, a month for life, by not staying for thirty years.

Nonetheless, my retirement ceremony was scheduled for July 29, 2009. It was a beautiful, picturesque San Diego afternoon and everyone was gathered under white tents facing the San Diego Bay. My wife and nephew Stephen were in attendance, but my sons were unable to attend due to military obligations. I tried to get my mother to fly out for the retirement, but she wasn't going to leave Augusta. The woman who inspired me to love traveling seemed to have developed a phobia of leaving the Hill, but my Marine Corps family and my fraternity brothers were there. The Marine Corps opened many doors for me and my family, and now I was transitioning back to the civilian world with marketable skillsets I could use the rest of my life. I thank God for the journey. My family has a proud tradition of military service, evidenced by our presence in every branch of the military except the Coast Guard. My oldest son served in the Air Force for fifteen years and was deployed four times to Afghanistan and Iraq. My youngest served in the Air Force for eight years. I am proud of all my family members that are still serving and those that have served our nation in uniform for four generations. My official last day on active duty was October 1, 2009, and I retired at the rank of Master Gunnery Sergeant (E-9) at forty-three years old.

Goodness is about character-integrity, honesty, kindness, generosity, moral courage, and the like. More than anything else, it is about how we treat other people.
—Dennis Prager

WARRIOR TO TROJAN

WHILE VISITING THE base education office at Marine Corps Recruit Depot in San Diego (MCRD), I ran across an intriguing pamphlet for University of Southern California that talked about mental health social work, and they were offering sub-concentration in military and veteran services. Before that day, I was sure that I was going to work in sales upon retiring, but I was very interested in what I read about the possibility of helping people with a range of mental health challenges, including trauma and PTSD. My father's older brother, Elbert Ford, was a Marine and served in the Korean War. Uncle Elbert returned to the states and never spoke of his experiences, but it was clear that he was having difficulty adjusting (PTSD). He worked in New York City for most of the first ten years after coming home, then after a difficult breakup with his girlfriend, he returned to Washington, D.C. to see his mother, my paternal grandmother. My uncle had come home to say goodbye to my grandmother, and tragically, he committed suicide by ingesting rat poison in front of her. He was thirty-seven years old.

In July of 2009, I met Dr. Jose Coll, a Marine Corps Veteran and the first Director of the USC School of Social Work San Diego Academic Center.

He recruited me into the program, then after finding out what I did in the Marine Corps my last fifteen years, he offered me a job as the San Diego Academic Center's first recruiting coordinator. Dr. Coll and I forged one of the best working relationships I had ever experienced up until that point. We both came from humble beginnings, we were enlisted Marines, and we both shared a passion for helping students, both civilian and veteran affiliated. At my retirement, Dr. Paul Maiden, Vice Dean of the USC School of Social Work at the time, made the big announcement. "Today, Isaac is a Warrior, but Monday morning, he will be a USC Trojan." It was a wonderful, yet somber day as some of the most important people in my life looked on: my wife, nephew (Stephen), who was visiting from Atlanta, my lifelong Marine Corps family, and my fraternity brothers of Zeta Sigma Lambda Chapter, Alpha Phi Alpha Fraternity, Inc.

I was a long way from the Bottom. My Marine Corps career was ending after twenty-five years of faithful service, and I was literally starting a job at USC less than three days after retirement. Dr. Paul Maiden, the Executive Vice Dean at the time, asked to speak during my ceremony, and he called me out in front of the formation to present me with a signed USC football. Every time a door closed for me over the years, another bigger door opened. I began grad school a month after starting work; it was a dream transition from the military. The experience I built as a career recruiter in the Marine Corps over my last fifteen years, made me uniquely qualified to grow USC San Diego Academic Center enrollment. We grew the program from twenty-five students in its first year in August 2009 to over 200 students by the time I left USC in January 2016.

During my time at the school, I was promoted to Assistant Director of Military and Diversity Outreach for the School of Social Work. In this role, I recruited for the University Park Campus, Orange County Academic Center, San Diego Academic Center, and served as a veteran reintegration specialist for the school. I also counseled military- and veteran-affiliated students, conducted national outreach, veteran health workshops, and panel discussions for female and LGBT veterans, and contributed to the school's retention efforts. It was a dream job due to its blended nature. I didn't obtain supervised hours during these years toward licensure, but the job combined many aspects that

I was passionate about: under-represented minorities, transitioning veterans and their families, and mentorship. I juggled classes, internships, and a hectic, challenging travel schedule for three years. I was initially told that I couldn't work full-time and complete the school's challenging MSW program, and that was just what I needed to hear. In the Marine Corps the word *can't* didn't exist, and my favorite motto was "Make it happen."

I guess not sleeping for more than three hours a night since returning from the first Gulf War came in handy. My combined work and school schedule often lasted twelve to fourteen hours. I heard the voices of naysayers past. It was also not lost on me that I blew my first opportunity to complete my formal education decades earlier, and now I was commuting ninety miles round trip daily, and often flying more than five times a month during the peak recruiting season. As I traveled around the country, I would send mom postcards from every city. She said that she was able to travel with me through the many cards, letters, and souvenirs I would send her. I was determined that I would succeed both as a student and employee, even if it killed me. And I was going to bring as many people with me as possible. In between semesters, I would travel throughout the state and I took cruises.

My aunt Louise and Uncle Curtis from Baton Rouge, Louisiana, joined my wife and I on a cruise in 2011. While sitting in the ship's dining room for dinner, I imagined what it would be like to take a cruise with my mother and father. I was in a position to show my mother things she once dreamed of when she was younger, but now she was adverse to travel outside of Augusta. This wouldn't stop me from trying, though. I was determined to get my mother on a plane to California, so I could show her the iconic sights like Hollywood, the Golden Gate Bridge, La Jolla Cove, Balboa Park, and take her whale watching off the coast of San Diego. I remembered what my mother tried to do for us before alcoholism clouded her judgement, and I thank her to this day for my love of travel and exploration. I just wanted her to know that I still had good memories of her in my childhood.

In 2010, Gary Sinise of CSI New York and a tireless advocate of all things military and veteran, announced that he would be sponsoring a $10,000 inaugural scholarship for a service-connected veteran graduate student who was also an advocate for the military and veteran-affiliated community. Mr. Sinise was the new Bob Hope due to his tremendous support of all things military and for military families. I submitted the names of at least seven deserving veteran students who I thought were great candidates for the scholarship, and the school informed me that I would be honored as the first recipient of the Gary Sinise Scholarship due to my dedication to the intersection of social work and veterans causes. The scholarship was being presented at a combined recognition ceremony, A Celebration of the Heart, on Saturday, April 2, 2011 at the beautiful USC Town and Gown Hall. Also receiving awards at this event were Stephen Peck with the W. June Simmons Distinguished Alumni Award; Gary Sinise for outstanding community service and humanitarian efforts on behalf of the U.S. Military; and Fred H. Wulczyn for exceptional scholarship and the commitment to the profession of social work. Tickets were $200 each and my wife and I were honored to be attending such an event.

I was asked to speak during the ceremony and afterward, my wife and I took pictures with Gary Sinise and John Voight, Angelina Jolie's father. The University of Southern California School of Social Work really knew how to put on a production. The school not only offered me a world-class education, but I gained priceless relationships and was able to positively affect the lives of hundreds of students, both civilian and military. For this, I will forever be grateful. In April of 2012, after completing all the requirements for graduation, I called my mother to invite her to my May 12, 2012 commencement service. She had missed my graduation from boot camp, every promotion I received in the Marine Corps (E-1 through E-9), my graduation from National University in 2007, my retirement from the Marines in 2009, and many award ceremonies. My mother rarely traveled more than fifteen miles from her home over the last twenty years. I told her that I wanted to fly her out to see me graduate with my master's degree, and she told me that she was going to think about it because she hadn't flown in over thirty years. What I would find out a day after the vice dean announced that I was being promoted to Assistant Director of Military and Diversity Outreach that my mother was keeping a life-changing secret during the same time.

I've learned that people will forget what you said, people will forget what you did, but people will never forget how you made them feel.
—Maya Angelou

GRADUATION DAY

THE NIGHT BEFORE the main graduation, my wife, Aunt Louise, and Uncle Curtis attended the African American Cultural Celebration (Black Grad), a must-attend for all black USC graduates, bachelors through PhDs. Dr. Corlis Bennett-McBride was the director at the time, and she ensured that the celebration was an epic event each year. Seeing all the black graduates and families, many being the first in their families to graduate from college, was a beautiful sight to behold. The event featured singers, drummers, comedy, spoken word, and strolling by all the Black Greek letter organizations. The university has similar celebrations the same night for Latino and Asian Pacific Island students. My family and I went to dinner and prepared for the main graduation the next day. The School of Social Work graduation ceremony took place in the world-famous Shrine Auditorium, the same venue that hosted the Academy Awards between 1988 and 2001 and the Grammys until 2000.

As I sat in this historic venue, minutes away from receiving my graduate degree, I reflected on my humble beginnings and how blessed I was to even be there. Unselfishly, my mother was keeping a secret, one that if I had known about may have delayed this day. She knew that knowledge of her illness would've caused me to be distracted and focus on her in Georgia, so she kept it to herself. As my row stood up to head to the stage, I called her on my cell phone. "Mom, you're here with me in spirit, and you will walk across the stage with me." It was one of the proudest moments of my life, and I could feel my mother beaming with pride through the cell phone, as my wife, Aunt Louise and Uncle Curtis looked on from the balcony. When my name was called, I walked proudly across that stage to not only receive my graduate degree, but I was receiving validation. This was a tremendous milestone for me, much bigger than anyone at USC could ever imagine. *I refused to allow anything to break me, and here I am,* I thought to myself. I no longer felt like I was "less than," or that I had to prove anyone wrong. Dean Flynn handed me my diploma and hugged me as the newest member of my village, and all the faculty, staff, and students that I considered my family looked on. Davitric, my oldest son, texted me a message that was the greatest graduation gift any father could receive.

"Thank you for letting me see what a man is supposed to be." This was the best compliment any father could ever hope for. I had asked God years ago to allow me to see my sons become men, and He did this and much more. We celebrated with family, fellow graduates, and my fraternity brothers over dinner at the Grand LUX Cafe in Los Angeles. Gwen and I took Aunt Louise and Uncle Curtis sightseeing on Saturday and Sunday before they headed back to Baton Rouge. I headed back to work the following Monday, anxious to start working in my new role. My two and a half years as a police officer, and my short stint working at the Augusta Regional Youth Development Center (RYDC) and Augusta Correctional Medical Institute, exposed me to hundreds of souls who found themselves on a drastically different path than I.

The short answer was that God had a different plan for me, and I believe He wanted me to be an example for those who may question whether there is light after darkness. I was proud of the work I did for USC, especially the work with underrepresented minorities, increasing the number of male social work students and transitioning veterans and families. My door was always open, and I practically lived at the school supporting students. Two days after the school-wide announcement went out about my promotion, faculty, staff, and student emails poured in congratulating me. My hard work was paying off, and I had accomplished my goal of creating a post-Marine Corps career, one that I loved. I was welcomed from the Marine Corps with opened arms, as an employee and student, and at one point, I thought that this would be my final stop.

Due to injuries sustained on active duty: chronic back pain, a lacerated bicep injury and torn rotator cup, my blood pressure began to spike. Physical pain was certainly a culprit, but secretly, I masked years of unresolved hurt, disappointment, and anger at what I endured as a child, on the police department, during my climb through the ranks of the Marine Corps, and my secret struggle with depression and PTSD. It all caught up with me, and on November 30, 2013, I suffered a transient ischemic attack (TIA). I was forty-eight years old, a health nut, stayed in shape, had never smoked, and I had a glass of wine or champagne on special occasions. No one was more shocked than my wife. Up until this incident, she believed I was indestructible because she had seen me survive so much. I went on medical leave and returned months later as if nothing had happened. Within that same year, I was selected as Top Staff Member of the Year by veteran students at the 2014 USC Black Grad Recognition Dinner.

I was recognized along with five other veterans working in higher education with a Top Veteran Influencer in Higher Education Award in Temecula, and I was selected as 2014 "Alpha Man of the Year" for Zeta Sigma Lambda Chapter, Alpha Phi Alpha Fraternity. I eventually left the university in December 2015, just short of six years, due to the school closing all three of the university's academic centers. I also made a paradigm change regarding my career goals. I decided that I would embrace being retired while working. And since I was a workaholic, I thought I should be one for my own businesses. I started Isaac Ford Jr. & Associates, LLC, which included real estate investing, photography (PhotosbyIsaac), recruiting and diversity solutions consulting, authorpreneur, and motivational speaking.

He giveth power to the faint; and to them that
have no might he increaseth strength
—Isaiah 40:29

MOM'S BIG SECRET

A FTER CALLING MY mother and not reaching her for several days, I asked my aunt Evelyn to stop by her house. She did, and reported that my mom didn't answer the door, something she would do to her sisters from time to time. I asked my aunt to call local hospitals because it was unlike her to not answer my calls. She did, and discovered that my mother had been admitted to University Hospital. She was treated, and she was trying to get neighbors to pick her up from the hospital because she didn't want her relatives to see her. Red flags went up immediately because there were close to fifty relatives in Augusta that she could've called. We have a very close-knit family, very responsive to the needs and welfare of our aunts and uncles. During this same time, we discovered that my mother had fallen and was on the floor of her home for three days before neighbors heard her calls for help. The Augusta Fire Department had to break-in to rescue her.

My sister lived in Atlanta, my brother lived in Savannah, and I was living on the west coast, yet still, an aunt, niece, or nephew could always reach my mother in an emergency within twenty minutes. We had no idea that she was sick based on recent telephone calls. When family members went by to check on her after she was released from the hospital, she wouldn't let them in. She told my aunts and cousins to leave things on the porch. Each time they visited her over a period of weeks, she spoke to them through a cracked door. She never mentioned anything to me and kept it all to herself. My brother traveled from Savannah to investigate and as soon as he saw her he called me. "You need to come home. Mom is not looking good," he said. "Mom has lost a lot of weight, come home as soon as you can."

He took pictures of some medical papers he found lying around during his visit and sent them to my sister-in-law. She works in medical billing and confirmed that the codes coincided with oncology. Three days later, my siblings and I were with my mother during her oncology appointment at University Hospital. As soon as the oncologist entered the exam room, I greeted him with a question."What is going on with our mother?" He looked away from me and looked at my mother in a scolding manner.

"What did I tell you, Ms. Ford?"

"You said you were running some more tests," she replied.

"No, I told you that you have pancreatic cancer and it's terminal." I didn't like his tone, but it was clear that she was in denial and they had discussed her diagnoses over quite some time. We expected the worst given that this appointment was with an oncologist, but still it was shocking to finally hear those words come out of his mouth. It felt like a bad dream I wanted to wake up from. "I hate you!" she blurted out to the doctor in anger. It was official. Now I understood why she didn't want to fly out to Los Angeles for my retirement or graduation. Now we understood why she was avoiding relatives that stopped by to see her and insisted that they place things on the front porch. "How long does our mother have to live?" I asked the doctor. "She has about two months." I instinctively went into therapist mode with her, wanting to know if she were afraid, in which she was."We are too," I said. "But we are here for you, and we are going to get through this together."

My mother kept her cancer diagnosis a secret for more than a year. It now made sense, why she would say, "At least I'm not in any pain." I never understood what she meant by that cryptic statement during our weekly calls. We had not seen her look so vulnerable, so afraid since we were children. Our mother was always fearless, but this understandably terrified her and us. I wondered was she afraid of the chemotherapy treatments. *Did the oncologist tell her that treating pancreatic cancer was futile? Why didn't she try to undergo some type of treatments?* We soon found out that my mother's cancer had metastasized, spreading to her liver and colon.

I couldn't imagine getting such news and feeling helpless to fight it. My sister had spent the previous week with mom, waiting on her and caring for her. My brother drove up and stayed with me at the house for a couple of days. I took mom to additional doctor appointments and ran errands with her. We went to my cousin Cassandra's beauty salon to get her hair done. She craved lemons and salt, and we bought scratch-off lottery tickets, her favorite pastime, outside of reading current events. She was very frail and had lost a significant amount of weight. Her gaunt appearance was hard to believe. I carried her up the stairs of her front porch, because she was too weak to navigate them alone. My three aunts lovingly held a vigil at her home day and night, trying to assist my mother as much as possible. They loved her, and she loved them. She was known for being tough on them, but they wouldn't be deterred.

They would eventually go home, but they would be right back the next day before noon. Every time she got up at night, I was right there behind her, afraid that she would fall because she was so weak. She couldn't sleep and neither could I. It was hard to imagine what was going through her mind in these last days. I rarely got more than three hours of sleep anyway, so I had no problem listening for her if she needed me. I watched over her like a mother with a newborn would, and watched helplessly as my mother became weaker by the day. She couldn't even open a bottle of water or open the door, yet she refused to allow her sisters to help her. Mom wouldn't agree to hospice, and she didn't want to leave the Hill at this point. I called the EMS to do a wellness check and she passed the series of questions with flying colors.

We sat on the porch each night because she couldn't sleep, and I wanted her to be able to talk about her thoughts, fears, and wishes. My mother adored her grandchildren and great-grands, especially her newest great granddaughter, though she had only seen pictures of her. My youngest son and his wife were both in the Air Force at the time, and they were stationed in Abilene, Texas, so she hadn't seen my one-year-old granddaughter in person yet. My mother purchased a beautiful red winter coat for the baby, but it was still too big for her to wear. My wife and I were saving it for her until she was big enough to wear it.

As I began to update her on the baby's progress, she grew angry with every picture I showed her of my granddaughter. "I don't want to hear about no damn baby." I abruptly stopped talking about her, because it was clear that my mother was still in the anger stage of dying, and I let her know that I understood why she was angry and how difficult it must've been. She was angry because she knew she would never get to hold her great-granddaughter. She would never see her wear the red coat she had bought for her, and she wouldn't get to see her grow up. My mother was very proud of her grandchildren, and now she wouldn't get to see any of her six great-grands grow any further. I told her that we could discuss anything she wanted to or not talk at all, so we just sat in silence, watching the cars drive by on this hot, muggy, July night.

My mother was a lifelong member of Thankful Baptist Church, but she requested that her funeral be held at a small church on Royal Street.

"I want my friends on the Hill to be able to attend my funeral, so I want my funeral to be held at the church down the street."

"Okay, Mom. I will contact the church and do my best to secure it for your service."

"Who do you want to preach your funeral?"

"Steve!" she said. "I want my nephew to preach my funeral."

I reached out to the church down the street and offered to pay for everything, but they rejected my dying mother's request to be funeralized in her neighborhood church due to church politics. I was pissed. My faith was still strong, but I had a serious problem with a church making such a heartless decision. My cousin, Steve, stopped by to see my mother; he prayed with her and he agreed to preach at her funeral. It is a very difficult thing to discuss impending death and funeral arrangements with a loved one. But our close relationship, my strong faith in God, and my clinical training helped me get through this very difficult time.

My mother couldn't safely stay in her home, but to take her to the hospital against her wishes would be considered kidnapping. All of my aunts were on hand before I left for Atlanta, and my mother smiled because she would be able to stay at home for now. I climbed on her bed, kissing her all over her face, as she swatted me away in a playful manner. I was happy that I was able to make her smile before I left town, and my aunts assured me that they would look out for her when I left. I told my mother I loved her, that I had to go, but I would be back soon. This would be the last time I would ever see my mother alive.

Forgiveness is not an occasional act.
It is a permanent attitude.
—Dr. Martin Luther King Jr.

ALL IS FORGIVEN

ALTHOUGH WE OFTEN hesitate when it comes to forgiving others, the desire to be forgiven is universal. "If you forgive those who sin against you, your Heavenly Father will forgive. But if you refuse to forgive others, your Father will not forgive your sins." (Matthew 6:14-15) When the Apostle Peter came to Jesus and asked, "Lord, how often should I forgive someone who sins against me? Seven times?"

"No!" Jesus replied. "Seventy times seven!" (Matthew 18: 21-22) How people define forgiveness is as varied as opinions about religion or politics, but ultimately it involves our decisions about relinquishing feelings of revenge or resentment. We may never forget what people say or do to us, and that's okay. But when we forgive, we escape the control yielded by those who caused us harm. This is what allows us to be at peace, to move on from the hurt, and on with our lives. Releasing our pent-up anger and bitterness also helps us to have better health and peace of mind. Forgiveness can lead to healthier relationships, improved mental health, less anxiety, stress and hostility, lower blood pressure, fewer symptoms of depression, a stronger immune system, improved heart health, and improved self-esteem. (Rakel 2018)

For many years, I planned to ask my mother for the long overdue apology I never received as a child. I always wanted to hear her say, "I'm sorry, Son." But by the time my plane landed in Atlanta, I had already decided that it was less important now. I no longer needed her to say it because I knew she loved me, and I loved her unconditionally. It was now more important than ever that I told my mother that all was forgiven. I am grateful for the close bond we had for decades after the tragedy and for that precious last week I was able to spend with her before returning to California. My mother always loved me and my siblings. But given our complicated past, some wondered out loud how I could have such a relationship with my mother. One of my aunts once said to me, "I don't know what you are, but I will never forget the way you loved your mother." She didn't understand how I got through the things I did, and how I could be so forgiving and loving toward her. For me, it was pretty simple.

The Bible didn't say "Honor thy father and mother if they were perfect." It says, "Honor thy father and thy mother," that "thy days may be long upon the land which the Lord thy God giveth thee." (Exodus 20:12) So, I did. My prayer was that neither my mother nor I would be defined by what happened so many years earlier, and that our example of unconditional love would be a model for others in similar situations, proof that anything is possible if you have faith. I had to return to California on the fifth of July, called my mother daily, and had planned to return within another week or so.

But after a second fall at the house that caused her to be hospitalized for five days, my mother had finally agreed to hospice care. We were all relieved that she was in a safe place where she could receive the level of care she deserved. After returning home, I spoke with her the next day as she was sitting on the side of the bed reading her newspapers. She loved current events as I did. We discussed the news of the day and her appetite. She sounded like herself, barely a hint that she was so gravely ill. When I called the following day, the nurse went to wake her up so she could take my call. This time, the conversation was more one-sided, and I could sense that she was weaker and less engaged. "I love you," I said. "Get some rest and I will call you later." I wanted to be by her side, and I really regretted not heading back to Augusta earlier, but I didn't want to see her suffer at the end. I had seen death up close many times before, in many settings, but I didn't want to watch my mother die. Before I got the courage to return to Augusta, my mother entered the last phase of her journey.

My brother and sister, and my mother's sisters were by her bedside when she made her transition. My brother called me the last night of her life at about 6:00 p.m. and described the scene of soft, spiritual music playing with mom resting with family by her side, and the hospice staff, including the Chaplain, on hand. What my big brother was really describing was our mother being actively in the dying process. "Send me a picture of Mom," I said. My brother was reluctant, but I wanted to see her and needed to say my final goodbye. I asked my brother to put the telephone to my mother's ear, and he did. "I love you so much, Mom. It's okay. I love you, I forgive you, and I will see you later." This was my last opportunity to say, "I forgive you." I felt relieved and at peace. I told my brother that I loved him, and I hung up. My wife was standing nearby, and I looked at her with tears in my eyes. "My mother will be gone by morning."

When my aunt Evelyn called me at about 5:00 a.m. the next morning to deliver the news, I was awake and waiting for the call. "Ike, your mother is gone." Within two days, I was in Augusta with my siblings making the arrangements for my mother's homegoing. I walked into the funeral home with my wife and siblings, pausing at the door before continuing into the funeral home chapel. It felt like something was pushing me back. I composed myself then continued into the room displaying her body. She looked like she was sleeping, and I was pleased with the dress my sister selected for her burial. This was real. My mother was really gone just weeks before her sixty-eighth birthday. For years, my siblings and I believed that alcohol would eventually kill our mother. I never imagined that cancer would take her. I didn't cry much, not because I didn't love her, but rather because I loved her while she lived. My mother loved all of us and we loved her unconditionally. Since I was in my late teens, I have believed in telling people how I feel about them in the present. I believed in giving flowers to my mother, aunts, wife, and even my granddaughter while they are alive. I feel like I did the right things by her, despite her mistakes. My mother had a beautiful ceremony attended by family and friends, not on the Hill as she requested, but like she wanted, it was preached by her nephew at his church.

For over thirty-five years following the incident, I honored her. I advocated for her. I loved her, and, most important, I forgave her. As imperfect as she was, she was my mother, the mother God wanted me to have. Through the love she demonstrated before and after that fateful Saturday morning, she was once again made whole and finally at peace. My mother gave birth to three resilient, loving, and accomplished children, who bore five beautiful, intelligent, and accomplished grandchildren and eight great-grandchildren. This was Lillie Mae's legacy.

The Lord is nigh unto them that are of a broken heart;
and saveth such as be of contrite spirit.
—Psalm 34:18

BIG IKE'S ABSENCE

B IG IKE, AS we called my father, had his own battles with racism while working as a supervisor with LabCorp in Washington, D.C. Through his siblings, I discovered that my father had a nervous breakdown in his forties and never worked a full-time job again, outside of briefly working as part-time apartment manager and taking photos in D.C. nightclubs (He even tried his hand as a freelance photographer.). I thought my love of photography came exclusively from my aunt Mildred in Augusta, but I actually got the shutter genes from him. My father was said to be one of the top lab technologists working for LabCorp, and he endured discrimination despite his qualifications and proven results. He was said to have supervised several white employees, something that few African Americans were doing in the early seventies.

After working for several years to earn a promotion as a lab supervisor, a young white trainee, who was trained by my father, was promoted over him and became his supervisor. This enraged my father, causing him to have a nervous breakdown and he walked off his job, never working in his field again. Years later, my aunt Onita, a brilliant retired civil service worker, assisted my father in appealing for retirement benefits based on the years he had already put in, and because his case was so egregious. To everyone's surprise, he was granted retirement benefits in 1991. Before he began receiving his pension, his sisters, and my aunt Onita's husband supported him financially, and my aunt Anne rented her basement apartment to him.

During the years that my father was absent from our lives, we had no knowledge that he was suffering from mental illness and was homeless. This explained some, but not all of my father's absence from 1973-1983. My father was gainfully employed and healthy during these crucial years, but he still didn't support us financially or emotionally. My father began showing early signs of Dementia in his early fifties. This terrified me for years, even though his siblings ranged in ages seventy-seven to ninety-three and are very active in their later years. Before his health began to decline, none of his siblings ever saw the inside of a nursing home. One of many things I wasn't aware of was that my father was robbed while leaving a nightclub that he was working. I learned that he was struck in the head with his camera, causing head injuries.

Perhaps this was the reason for his early memory concerns. His long-term memory was crisp, and he loved talking about the good ole days, including his childhood on the farm in Birmingham, his college days, his stint in the army, and fond memories of time spent with my sister and me in Washington, D.C. In reality, much of what he remembered never happened. My sister and I visited during an Upward Bound trip to Washington in 1982, and for my grandmother's funeral in 1997. My father never sent for us to spend time with him or our D.C. family after we left as small children. After leaving USC, working in medical social work greatly assisted me in my advocacy of my father as I wanted to get a better understanding of the challenges and resources available for aging parents with Alzheimer's and Dementia. I am also grateful to my aunts Jessica, Louise, Anne, Onita, and my cousins, Angie and Jeane, for helping my sister and me fill in the many missing pieces over the past twenty years. He checked out as a father when we were young, and he checked out of the working world in his forties.

My father's mental illness was yet another reason why I felt I had to work even harder to be successful. He was the fallen angel of his siblings. Out of the ten, eight had four-year degrees and three earned master's degrees. His oldest sister and biggest advocate believed he was the smartest of them all, and his high intelligence was his downfall. Decades later, I scolded my father for not knowing or caring about how we were fairing in Augusta. My father visited me while I was stationed at Marine Corps Recruit Depot (MCRD) San Diego in 2007. We spent four wonderful days sightseeing and catching up. This was the most time I had spent with my father since he visited my family in Augusta in 1997. I took him on tours of several Marine Corps and Naval bases in the area. We also visited Balboa Park, La Jolla Cove, Point Loma, Temecula Wine Country, and the museum ships along the San Diego Bay. "I forgive you, but I just need to understand why you couldn't be there," I said. "Son, I should have been more involved. I'm sorry. I want to try and have a relationship with you and your sister, my grandchildren, and great-grands." I thought that his absence was strictly due to apathy, that he was a deadbeat dad. That was certainly a big part of it for ten years, but my D.C. family knew better. They watched his tragic fall from grace up close. I began a nearly twenty-year pilgrimage back and forth, beginning in 2002 to seek answers about my father and his absence and to reconnect with my relatives.

I thank my father's siblings and my cousins for welcoming us back with open arms and for helping me to find the answers to my many questions. An uncle on my mother's side of the family told me years later that my maternal grandfather made the decision to not let my father know about the incident with me and my mother. My father didn't find out about it until I was in my mid-forties. Though my father's conversations focused on the olden days, he read extensively and loved to discuss current events too. During my visits to D.C., we would sit up late at McDonald's across the street from Howard University, and he would tell me about the incredible legacy the Black Harvard has had on our community and the nation. He told me that my sister and I were Freedman babies because we were born in Freedman's Hospital, Howard University's hospital. One night we were discussing poems I had to commit to memory. I was amazed that he could still recite the poem *Invictus*, word for word. I would recite a line, and he would complete the next. My father spent over thirty years holding court at Wendy's restaurant on Georgia Avenue. He would buy coffee, read several newspapers, and chat with customers. I shared his love for current events, politics, and we both loved to meet people and engage in intelligent debates. He was a fixture, so much so, everyone always knew where to find him—in his office.

My father's sight became increasingly worse due to glaucoma. While leaving the VA following an appointment, my father fell on the sidewalk, but luckily my aunt Onita, who accompanied him to all his appointments, was on hand. He was hospitalized following the fall and remained in the VA Hospital for two weeks. After being hospitalized in 2016, my father's health declined. Decades of chain smoking resulted in him developing severe chronic obstructive pulmonary disease (COPD), and his appetite and weight loss became a concern. While visiting him following his health scare, I obtained a medical power of attorney, something that was crucial given his worsening memory concerns. My father was released from the hospital, and he initially stayed with my aunt Onita in Silver Spring, Maryland. After a few months, he insisted on renting an apartment of his own, not too far from my aunt Anne's home in D.C.

This was a huge mistake, because for the first time in many years, neither my aunt Anne nor Aunt Onita could ensure that he was taking care of himself. They had both supported my father for decades, preventing him from becoming homeless. In the year that my father rented this new apartment, he made a costly mistake by not taking his glaucoma eye drops. Chest pains led him to being hospitalized again, and I received the call at 2:30 a.m. from a physician at Holy Cross Hospital in Silver Spring, Maryland, stating that he needed emergency blood clot surgery. I authorized it, and they took care of the blood clots, but the anesthesia adversely affected his cognitive ability after the surgery. When I arrived in Maryland to see my father at Holy Cross Hospital, he was delirious and had to be placed in restraints; this was very painful to watch. We didn't know whether he would regain his previous level of cognitive ability, but after several days, my father returned to his previous level of cognitive ability.

While my father's siblings and I held a vigil in the ICU waiting room, an uncle shared with me something I had never heard before from his siblings. On each trip to D.C., I always quizzed someone about my father, about those missing years, about facts I could never get from him, and it was his time in the interview seat. He told me that during my father's healthy years, he admonished him about his lack of involvement in our lives; how he told him that he had children in Augusta and needed to be involved in our lives. Though painful to hear, I appreciated this moment of clarity and honesty. It was the first time that anyone had been honest enough to tell me that my father was selfish, and for many years while he was healthy, he didn't give a damn. In those first days after surgery, my father didn't know who any of us were, but soon he was back to his previous level of awareness. We also learned that his heart was only functioning at twenty percent. The attending physician asked me whether I wanted them to resuscitate him if that was needed and I said of course. I had never given up on him, not then, and I wouldn't now.

All of his siblings were by his bedside, and after several days, my father regained some of his cognitive ability, but things were changing. It was clear that my father would require full-time care, and he would need a facility with memory care for Alzheimer's/Dementia. He was transferred to Arcola Assisted Living Facility in the same city as the hospital. My aunt Onita, his oldest sister, helped me complete the application for long-term care medicaid. She was my boots on the ground from this point on. She is ninety years old and sharp as ever, a living angel. She accompanied my father to medical appointments, and visited him daily after he was placed in an assisted living facility. She ensured that the facility was attentive to my father's needs, and she took the time to read Bible verses to him each day.

We talked by phone weekly, and I mailed him pictures and showed him videos of his great-granddaughter during visits before he lost his sight completely. In June of 2018, my father was taken back to Holy Cross Hospital for the last time. My father again became delirious, and Arcola was unable to feed him, primarily due to the progression of his Dementia. By law, Arcola wasn't allowed to restrain patients, and they didn't have the staff to watch him, yet the hospital released him back to Arcola once again, but they couldn't feed him or keep him hydrated. Although he had lost a tremendous amount of weight, he was strong enough to be a danger to himself. Arcola no longer had the resources or staffing to ensure his safety, so I made the decision to place him in hospice care. Doctors informed me that my father had probably had a stroke or two, which contributed to his current condition. He was moved to Holy Cross Hospice where he was able to be sedated and appeared to be resting better. I swear by hospice, given the care they provided for both of my parents. On Tuesday, June 5, 2018, I had just finished a visit with a client when I got the call from my father's hospice physician updating me on his condition.

"Your father is actively in the dying process," she said. I didn't expect to hear that. His rapid decline didn't make sense, and I was hoping she was calling to tell me that he was doing better. "Dementia usually doesn't progress this fast," she said. I asked her to go to his room and put the telephone to his ear. She did, and held the telephone as I told my father the same thing I told my mother before her death. "I love you, I forgive you, and I will see you later."

My father fought for the next four days, and he transitioned at 11:00 p.m., on June 9, 2018, just shy of his eighty-first birthday. I made my father's funeral arrangements from California with the help of aunts and cousin Angie. I am grateful to my aunts, Onita and Anne, for everything they did for my father over the years and for helping me during his illness. I arrived in D.C. two days before my father's funeral, and my sister and I had to get my aunts to help with his obituary. There was still so much we didn't know, even after years of reaching out to him. I was still in the dark as to who he really was and what really happened to him. It was hard to get solid answers from him about certain chapters of his life (and ours) before his health declined.

I listened in amazement, as the preacher preached my father's funeral. He talked about my father's love of current events, how he could read two or three newspapers in one sitting (I could do the same thing); and how he spoke to everyone and mentored young people in the neighborhood, despite his absence in our lives. And, of course, he talked about his love for photography. Listening to the pastor talk about all the things Isaac Ford Sr. did made me feel like I was listening to my own funeral. We had a lot in common, yet we were opposites when it came to follow-through. Some of this was inexcusable, but there were many years that he was incapable of being present. I was no longer angry at him because I held his feet to the fire before his health failed. He apologized for not knowing what he should have known during the most challenging years of our childhood.

As with my late mother, I let him in and showed him love unconditionally. We needed him all those years, but he was still my father, and I was Isaac Ford Jr. My father was laid to rest at Quantico National Cemetery, just outside of Marine Corps Base Quantico in Northern Virginia. My father loved all things military, and on business trips to the area, he often accompanied me to Quantico Marine Base. We never discussed where he wanted to be buried, but I am sure he would've approved of the choice we made. The inscription on my father's tombstone reads: "Our beloved father, he lived his life with dignity."

Hope begins in the dark, the stubborn hope that if you just show up and try to do the right thing, the dawn will come. You wait and watch and work; you don't give up.
—Anne Lamott

BLOODIED BUT UNBOWED

I HAVE NEVER BELIEVED in coincidences, but rather that everything happens because there is a divine purpose. The chance encounter between my CPS caseworker and I in that San Diego hotel opened a floodgate of emotions that I had managed to mask for four decades, and gave me the courage to finally confront painful childhood memories and the residual scars, both physical and emotional, that have haunted me throughout my adult life. Some people are naturally resilient, while others experience post-traumatic growth, which is moving past traumatic events and experiences with help. My village is the essence of who I am and without them I could have become a statistic. They loved, affirmed, and carried me before I was strong enough to stand on my own. Throughout the years that followed, the trajectory of my life has been similar to that of an elevator.

With every obstacle that I successfully navigated, passage to another floor was granted. I convinced myself that anything was possible with hard work, sacrifice, determination, faith, and a relentless desire to live my best life. It allowed me to reflect on how blessed I am to have such a loving, nurturing family—and extended family (aka village), that saw me through some of the most difficult days of my childhood and life. The love and encouragement I received from them prepared me for the many challenges that awaited me years later, including in law enforcement, the Marine Corps, higher education, and as a business owner.

It is said that "only steel can strengthen steel," and in the Marine Corps, there is a famous slogan that speaks to inner strength: "Pain is weakness leaving the body." The adversity and tragedy I experienced in the Delta Manor Housing Projects tested me, but couldn't break me, because resilience and determination were ingrained in my DNA with every trial and tribulation I survived. The message of my story is that you can grow from anything, even the most daunting challenges, and you don't have to be defined by what happens to you. Remember, you are ultimately the master of your own fate, even if you start at the bottom. Write your own narrative and live your best life until the music stops.

PHOTO GALLERY

1st PLACE WINNERS from Paine College's Project Upward Bound program in annual PUB olympics are: top row (left to right) Tonia Mason, literary (short story); Sheila Smith and Eddie Smith, scrabble; and Audrey Mack, spelling bee. Bottom row (left to right) Issac Ford, individual speech (impromptu); Timothy Wilson, tennis; and Byron Johnson and Philip Crockett, chess.

Paine College Upward Bound in the 10th grade

Before the prom at Mom's (1983)

Kenny and Mary at my grandparents' house (1978-1980)

On patrol in the Bottom (1986)

Holding Isaac III before going
on patrol for the Augusta
Police Department (1987)

Desert Shield and Storm, Al Jubal,
Saudi Arabia (24 years old)

My wedding day
in Albany, Georgia
(March 1986)

Gwen, Davitric, Isaac III,
and I (1989-1990)

Davitric and Isaac III in
our new home (1994)

Cousin Valerie's wedding reception attended by family

My maternal
grandparents
and Aunt Olivia

My mom (about 27-30 years old) in Augusta, Georgia

My mom on Royal Street (2010)

Mary, Mom, and I (1980-1982)

East Hale Street in Delta Manor (the Bottom)

Our apartment in Delta Manor

Grandparents'
house in
the Bottom

Promotion to Master Gunnery Sergeant in San Diego (2007)

My final rank as Master Gunnery Sergeant before retirement (2009)

Marine Corps Ball at MCRD, San Diego before retirement

On the Hill with Mom (2010)

My D.C. Village (left to right) Anne, Onita, Elizabeth, Jessica, and Louise

Graduation
from
USC (2012)

My father and I at Aunt Onita's house (2016)

My village from the Bottom (left to right) Wallace
Sr., Myrtis, Sylvester, Evelyn, and Mildred

My siblings:
Kenny,
Mary, and I

My wife,
Gwen, and I
at the Holiday
Ball in San
Diego (2017)

ACKNOWLEDGMENTS

I am eternally grateful to my Lord and Savior Jesus Christ. Without your loving grace, I never would have seen this day. To my late mother, Lillie B. Ford, thank you for giving me life and for loving me the best way you knew how. To my late father, Isaac Ford Sr., thank you for giving me life. To my late grandparents: Mary Lee Boler and Mason Boler Sr., thank you for loving all of us and ensuring we got to the finish line. To my incredible siblings: Mary R. Crawford and Kenneth Boler, I love you more than you know, and I am immensely proud of you both. Everything was more bearable knowing you were there.

To my beautiful wife, Gwen, thank you for loving me unconditionally over the past three decades. You are an incredible mother and Nana. To my sons: Davitric Jackson and Isaac III, I love you and I am proud to be your father. To my precious granddaughter, Azalia, Papa loves you more than you will ever know. I am so proud to be your Papa. To my beautiful, loving aunts: Evelyn, Mildred, Myrtis, Louise, Anne, Onita, and my late aunts: Jessica and Elizabeth. Thank you for loving me, praying for me, and helping answer questions that eluded me for decades. And a special thank you to my uncles: Harold, Sylvester, my late uncle Charlie Joe, Wallace Sr., Bill, Charles, Billie, and Curtis. Thank you for being my father figures, big brothers, and mentors in my father's absence.

To my cousin, Sharrel, I remember the trips to Baskin-Robbins. Thank you for always affirming me. To my cousin, Valerie, thank you for always having an encouraging word in those difficult days and today. I remember.

A special thanks to my cousins: Marion, Wallace Jr., Robert Gross, Olander, Dwayne, Charon, Linda, Brenda, Miriam, Sheri, Shannon, Chaundrel, Cheryl, Richard, Stephen, Karen, and all of my Georgia cousins for being a part of my supportive network of extended family. To my cousins, Angie, Jeane, Vincent, Ricky, Denise, Shannon, and Lamar, thank you for going out of your way to reintroduce me to my D.C family.

Thank you to all of my teachers at A. R. Johnson Health Professions High School and my classmates, especially Freddie and Yogi, for keeping me updated over the years. Thank you to Mrs. Ernestine Harris and the Paine College Upward Bound Program. Your leadership and the Upward Bound Program gave me my first job and played an integral role in preparing me for life. Thank you to all of my professors and colleagues at the University of Southern California School of Social Work.

Thank you to Mrs. Ophelia Adams for being such a loyal friend in the wake of the Augusta Police Department. I love and appreciate you. Thank you, Barbara Krotzer and Captain Leonard Hart. I remember. To Barbara Gordon of the Metro County Courier, thank you for being the voice of Augusta's African American community and for allowing me to tell my story when no one else would. Thank you, Dr. Joseph Lowery (SCLC), Rev. Kenneth Martin, the late Rev. N.T. Young, Councilwoman Kathleen Beazley, and the late Mr. Ed McIntyre for supporting me when I didn't have a voice. I remember.

Thank you to my Marine Corps family: Colonel William Gillespie, USMC (Ret.), Lt. Col Hector Shepard, USMC (Ret.), Master Gunnery Sergeant Breon Haskett, PhD, USMC (Ret.), Master Gunnery Sergeant Yolonda McCoy, USMC (Ret.), Master Gunnery Sergeant Kevin Knight, USMC, First Sergeant Sam Bagwell, USMC, (Ret.), Master Sergeant Kevin Williams, USMC, (Ret.), Gunnery Sergeant Nikita Wallace, USMC, (Ret.), Semper Fi!

To my friend, mentor, and Marine brother, Jose Coll, PhD, I appreciate all you've done to support me over the years. We made our mark and brought a lot of kids and veterans with us. To Kim Finny, PsyD., thank you for all you do, including graciously agreeing to write a review for *Up From the Bottom*. I am blessed to have such a wonderful friend and mentor.

To Yvonette Powell, LCSW, EdD, thank you for your unconditional love and support over the years. To Jeane Simpson, EdD, thank you for your wonderful support and affirmation, and writing a wonderful review. Terrence Fitzgerald, PhD, thank you, brother for your friendship and leadership. Colonel David Rabb, LCSW, thank you for agreeing to write a review for this project and for your friendship. Donna L. Cook, PhD, thank you for graciously agreeing to write a review for this project and for the affirmation. To the brothers of Zeta Sigma Lambda Chapter, Alpha Phi Alpha Fraternity, Inc., thank you for being an extension of my family.

A special thanks to my editor, Lakia Brandenburg, for being such a wonderful mentor during the editing and production phases of this project. To Sade Burrell, thank you for your encouragement and for sharing all of your phenomenal contacts for this first book. Along the way, there were many that touched my life through some of the most consequential phases of my life—thank you!

ABOUT THE AUTHOR

Isaac Ford Jr., MSW, is the former Assistant Director of Military and Diversity Outreach for the University of Southern California School of Social Work, a Veteran Reintegration Specialist, and a 2012 MSW graduate of the University of Southern California School of Social Work. Mr. Ford was born in Washington, D.C. and grew up in East Augusta, Georgia (The Bottom). Mr. Ford is a retired U.S. Marine Corps Master Gunnery Sergeant and a combat veteran of Operations Desert Shield and Storm. He currently lives in Southern California and is the owner of Isaac Ford Jr. & Associates, LLC, specializing in sales and diversity consulting, real estate investing, photography, and motivational speaking. Isaac Ford Jr. is available for select readings and speaking engagements throughout the country. For more info., visit www.IsaacFord.org.

REFERENCES

Dienstbier, R.A. 1992. "Mutual Impacts of Toughening on Crises and Losses." *In Life Crises and Experiences of Loss in Adulthood*, edited by L. Montada, S.H. Filipp, and M.J. Lerner, 367-384. Hillsdale, NJ: Lawrence Erlbaum Associates Inc.

Rakel, David, ed. 2017. "Forgiveness." In Integrative Medicine, 4th ed. Philadelphia: Elsevier, Accessed Oct. 5, 2017 at https://www.clinicalkey.com.

Seery, M.D., E.A. Holman, and R.C. Silver. 2010. "Whatever Does Not Kill Us: Cumulative Lifetime Adversity, Vulnerability, and Resilience." *J Pers Soc Psychol 99: 1025-1041.*

FINDING STUDIES

https://www.aa.org/

https://www.alz.org/

https://www.cancer.org

https://www.copdfoundation.org/

https://www.mayoclinic.org/disease-conditions/grand-mal-seizure/.../syc-20363458

https://www.webmd.com/mental-health/post-traumatic-stress-disorder

https://www.apa.org/helpcenter/road-resilience.aspx

GLOSSARY: CLINICAL AND MILITARY TERMS

Alcoholics Anonymous (AA): A fellowship of men and women who share their experiences, strengths, and hopes as they work toward recovery.

Alzheimer's Disease: Disorder that usually starts in middle age or later, resulting in progressive memory loss, impaired thinking, disorientation, and changes in personality and mood.

clear the net: A clearing of radio channels by a police dispatcher when an officer needs assistance.

Chronic Obstructive Pulmonary Disease (COPD): Umbrella term for progressive lung diseases, including emphysema, chronic bronchitis, and refractory (non-reversible) asthma. Eventually leads to increasing breathlessness.

delayed-entry program: Program used to prepare military enlistees before boot camp.

dementia: Condition in which memory and another cognitive function are affected severely enough to interfere with a person's ability to carry out daily activities.

drill instructor: Military trainer responsible for transforming military recruits into soldiers, sailors, airmen, marines, and coast guardsmen while in boot camp.

E-9: Highest enlisted rank in the US military.

Exceptional Family Member Program (EFMP): Mandatory enrollment program operated in conjunction with other agencies to provide comprehensive and coordinated community support, housing, educational, medical, and personal services to families with special needs.

geo-bachelor: Service member living separately from his or her family while stationed in the States.

grand mal seizure: Medical event in which a loss of consciousness and violent muscle contractions are caused by abnormal electrical activity throughout the brain.

hospice: Care that focuses on quality of life rather than length, usually occurring when death is predicted in six months or less.

ICU: Intensive care unit.

Master Gunnery Sergeant: One of two E-9 ranks in the Marine Corps.

military occupational specialty (MOS): Military technical skill or job.

mission-oriented protective posture (MOPP): Gas masks and protective clothing worn by military service members during nuclear, biological, and chemical warfare attacks.

post-traumatic stress syndrome (PTSD): Mental health condition in which a sufferer mentally relives a terrifying event on a repeated basis.

resilience: Adapting well in the face of adversity, trauma, tragedy, threats, or significant sources of stress. Bouncing back from difficult experiences.

service group life insurance (SGLI): Term life insurance carried by military service members while on active duty, currently valued at $400,000.

transient ischemic accident (TIA): Temporary blockage of blood flow to the brain, possibly signaling a full-blown stroke ahead.

RESOURCES

Adult Children of Alcoholics (ACOA): Self-help, self-supporting program to assist adults raised in alcoholic or otherwise dysfunctional families. (310) 534-1815, https://adultchildren.org

Al-Anon: Support group for family members of people with drinking problems. (757) 563-1600, https://al-anon.org

Alcoholics Anonymous: International fellowship of people battling alcoholism. (212) 870-3440, https://www.aa.org

Alpha Kappa Alpha Sorority Inc.: Organization that cultivates and encourages high scholastic and ethical standards, promotes unity and friendship among college women, and studies issues relating to girls and women. The group works to help women improve their social stature and maintain a progressive interest in college life. (773) 684-1282, www.aka1908.com

Alpha Phi Alpha Fraternity: Organization committed to the development and mentoring of youth and providing service and advocacy for the African American community. The fraternity develops leaders while promoting brotherhood and academic excellence. (410) 554-0040, www.apa1906.net, 2313 Saint Paul St. Baltimore, MD 21218

Angel Tree Program: Nationwide program through which church volunteers purchase and deliver gifts to children in the name of their imprisoned parents. 1-800-55-ANGEL.

Barrios Unidos: Program to prevent and curtail violence among youths in California's Santa Cruz County by providing them with life-enhancing alternatives. (831) 457-8208, www.barriosunidos.net

Black Star Project: Program seeking to increase the involvement of fathers and other positive male role models of color in the lives of children. (773) 285-9600, www.blackstarproject.org

Boys and Girls Clubs of America: Organization that seeks to inspire and enable all young people to realize their full potential as productive, responsible, and caring citizens. https://www.bgca.org

Children's Institute—Project Fatherhood: Project that aims to give fathers the tools to actively participate in rearing their children and helping them to thrive. Los Angeles, CA (213) 385-5100.

Daddy's Promise: Program designed to focus the attention of the African American community on the positive relationship that can and should exist between fathers and daughters. http://edgordon.net/daddyspromise.htm

DAV: Organization supporting veterans with rides to medical appointments, assistance with jobs and benefits, and more. www.dav.org

Delta Sigma Theta Sorority Inc.: Organization of college-educated women committed to the development of its members and to public service with a primary focus on the black community. (202) 986-2400, www.deltasigmatheta.org

Denver Urban Scholars: A program to help youth in the Denver metropolitan area pursue career and college opportunities. (303) 355-1700, www.denverurbanscholars.org

District of Columbia College Success Foundation: Organization seeking to provide students with educational and financial incentives, mentoring, and other support necessary to gain admission to college. Washington, DC, (202) 207-1800, www.dccollegesuccessfoundation.org

Family Counseling Center of the CSRA: Center providing professional counseling services to retired and active members of the military as well as all residents of the Central Savannah River Area, regardless of their ability to pay. Counseling is done individually as well as with families and other groups. Services focus on mental health, substance abuse, and family and other relationships. This organization also assists families going through the adoption process. (706) 868-5011, www.fcccsra.org

Foster Care Support Services Bureau: Bureau handling the temporary placement of children with supportive foster families when birth parents cannot care for them. (916) 651-7465, https://www.cdss.ca.gov/inforesources/Foster-Care

Freedom House Reentry Education and Employment Corp.: Organization to mentor and provide resources and support to formerly incarcerated individuals. The goal is to reduce the nation's staggering recidivism rate. 1-833-782-FREE.

Fulfillment Fund: Organization to mentor, counsel, and guide disadvantaged high school students toward achieving a college education. (323) 939-9707, Los Angeles, CA, www.fulfillment.org

Gay-Straight Alliance (GSA) Network: Youth leadership organization that connects school-based GSAs to one another and to community resources. California. (415) 552-4229

Georgia Crisis and Access Line: Twenty-four-hour assistance for mental health, drug, and other emergencies. 1-800-715-4225

Harmony Recovery Center: Center for substance-abuse treatment. Charlotte, NC. (866) 527-9131.

Hope House Inc.: Residential treatment facility that serves women eighteen and older who suffer from substance-abuse and mental-health disorders. Hope House serves three categories of individuals: homeless single women, pregnant women, and women with children, many of whom are seeking to regain custody of their children. (706) 737-9879, www.hopehouseaugusta.org

Jack & Jill of America Inc.: Organization made up of mothers with children ages two to nineteen, dedicated to nurturing future African American leaders by strengthening children through developmental activities. https://inlandempirejackandjill.org

Kappa Alpha Psi Fraternity Inc.: Organization that encourages honorable achievement in every field of human endeavor while promoting the spiritual, social, intellectual, and moral welfare of its members. (215) 228-7184, www.kappaalphapsi1911.com

National Child Abuse Prevention Partner Organizations: Organization through which federal agencies can share information on issues regarding child abuse and neglect. https://www.acf.hhs.gov/cb/resource/fediawg

National Suicide Prevention Lifeline: Network providing twenty-four hour free and confidential support to those in crises. 1-800-273-8255

Omega Psi Phi Fraternity Inc.: Fraternity with a mission to bring together college men with similar high ideals of scholarship and manhood for the purpose of stimulating new ideas and encouraging ambition. (404) 284-5533 www.oppf.org

100 Black Men of America: A men's civic organization and service club whose stated goal is to educate and empower African American children and teens. (404) 688-5100

Paine College Upward Bound Program: Program established in 1967 as the TRIO program to serve low-income and first-generation college-bound students. It includes rigorous academic instruction, tutoring, mentoring, counseling, and cultural enrichment activities. bedwards@paine.edu, (706) 821-8210.

Paralyzed Veterans of America: Organization that advocates for veterans who have experienced spinal cord injury or dysfunction. www.pva.org

Phi Beta Sigma Fraternity Inc.: Fraternity that promotes brotherhood, scholarship, and service, championing the idea of "Culture for Service and Service for Humanity." (202) 726-5434, www.phi beta sigma 1914.org

Raising Him Alone: A campaign to advocate for single mothers raising boys. (877) 339-4300 www.raisinghimalone.com

Sigma Gamma Rho Sorority Inc.: Organization with a mission to enhance the quality of life for women and their families in the United States and globally through community service and civil and social action. (919) 678-9720, www.sgrho1922.org

Smart Recovery: Nonprofit that helps people fight addictions through self-empowerment and self-reliance. (866) 951-5357, https://www.smartrecovery.org

The Links Incorporated: Corporation with a six-decade-long tradition of mentoring and preparing black children for bright futures. National. (202) 842-8686, www.linksinc.org

The Morehouse Male Initiative: Organization that promotes the affirmative development of African American males and disseminates research on the topic. Atlanta, GA

The Tom Joyner Foundation: Foundation that provides academic opportunities to students who attend or wish to attend historically black universities. www.tomjoynerfoundation.org

Pazzaz, Inc. Educational Enrichment Program: Provides educational services, including reading, writing, preparation for the high school equivalency test, English language, math, computers/technology. Also supports the Alpha Male program. Zoneice Jones is the primary contact: 619-264-6870, zoe@pazzaz.org.

US Department of Veterans Affairs: Department whose purpose centers on benefits and services for veterans. www.va.gov

Zeta Phi Beta Sorority, Inc.: Sorority committed to fostering the ideas of service, charity, scholarship, civil and cultural endeavors, sisterhood, and finer womanhood. (202) 387-3103, http:www.zphib1920.org